SOCIALIST BINGO:
Knowledge Distorted Journey

SOCIALIST BINGO:
Knowledge Distorted Journey

Germinal Boloix

Germinal Boloix
2017

Copyright © 2017 by Germinal Boloix
All rights reserved. This book or any portion thereof may not be reproduced or used in any manner whatsoever without the express written permission of the author except for the use of brief quotations in a book review or scholarly journal.

First Printing: 2017

ISBN 978-0-9958612-3-7

Germinal Boloix
email: gboloix@hotmail.com
Blog: gboloix.blogspot.com

Dedication

To my wife Erlinda. With her help during my convalescent months it was possible to complete the book.

Contents

Germinal Boloix 3
Acknowledgements 9
Preface 11
Introduction 15
Chapter 1: Starting the Journey 19
Chapter 2: Small Venice 'Paradise' 28
Chapter 3: Beach Town Resort 33
Chapter 4: Traveling to Beach Town 44
Chapter 5: Democracy at Pleasure Valley 51
Chapter 6: Society at Liberator Square 60
Chapter 7: Politics at Central University 72
Chapter 8: Devil's Advocate 82
Chapter 9: Marxism at The Institute 91
Chapter 10: Green Tablecloth Restaurant 100
Chapter 11: Bingo at Beach Town 111
Chapter 12: Back to the Future 119
Chapter 13: In Defense of the Lost Revolution 129
Chapter 14: Difficult Times for the Regime 139
Chapter 15: Aftermath of Harsh Times for The People 149
Final Notes 160
Epilogue 166

Acknowledgements

I want to thank all those that in a way or another inspired the making of this book. Likewise, to all the libraries and coffee shops that welcomed me during so many hours of writing.

Preface

The book presents the difficulties of a common citizen during his visits to 'Small Venice,' a country in South America. Most events are localized primarily in a small town called Beach Town, at the North-East of the country, near the Caribbean Coast. It presents a strong critique against Absurd Socialism, a political regime that promotes collective ownership of all production facilities in the name of The People. The State thinks it is in charge of executing policies in the name of the collectivity. The book presents journeys of knowledge search. That knowledge is distorted, it is not universal, it depends on the cultural and contextual conditions. Besides, every individual thinks different, it is difficult to agree.

Another aspect, inspiring the title of the book, is that Small Venice has been administered as an informal Bingo Organization. Socialists keep writing proclamations here and there (equivalent to calling numbers, finding patterns and defining winners) managing the resources of the country like their own private funds; winners are the closest allies of the regime, losers are The People.

Writing a book with lots of information doesn't attract readers, after a few pages they abandon. However, there is a need to produce stories charged with knowledge; pure and simple entertainment is worthless, it only kills time. Instead, providing knowledge and entertainment creates a useful mix that helps readers to build criteria. Interacting with personages and ideas, readers enrich their knowledge base. With very simple arguments, it is possible to understand more complex concepts. However, most of the time people do not read, those that need the knowledge to make decisions are not interested in learning; humanity is not progressing for lack of reading habits.

The story only covers a few aspects of a society, particularly its relationship with politics. Capitalism and socialism are two opposite views, related to the distribution of resources in a society, that fight for hegemony in the modern world. Democracy is a form of organization of the society that allows many strategies to be laid down for the good of the population.

In the same way that Karl Marx wrote a book against Capitalism, this book emphasizes Socialist defects. Marx wrote a book too difficult to understand; it is hoped that this one would be simpler to capture reader's interested in getting more knowledge. For those lovers of socialism, transport yourselves 170 years back in time, when Marx wrote his famous book, what capitalists thought about his book? Probably the same socialists would feel about this one. The author promotes the start of a scientific approach to determine objectively the good and bad aspects of socialism; primarily avoid socialism as an option.

Inspiration is a good feeling. You have some preoccupations and suddenly you find the answer to your doubts. It is a matter of putting ideas together, organizing and complementing. In some cases, you start building up a story from an initial idea, other times you build the libretto with all the elements incorporated from the beginning following a more precise plan. When you start with an idea, the beginnings include a few elements of the libretto, you start adding up new elements until the final work is completed. The inspiration for the book came after playing a few Bingo games with neighbors in an unknown beach town resort. The author found out, through these interactions, conversations, and dialogues, how people used to think and behave in different situations. The initial ideas were the nutshell of a cascade of topics that were included in the final version of the story.

The dialogues are invented, presenting arguments in favor and against political approaches. Most anecdotes and descriptions are inspired by real events but adapted according to the viewpoint of the main character; the story is fiction. The daily experiences of the author and the reality of the country have been used to invent a story with a resemblance to the truth. It is left at readers discretion to identify what is real and what is imaginary. The names of characters are invented, but inspired on real people, they left a nice souvenir and the author was thinking about them when writing. It has to be clear that the book is not a documentary, although some might think the events are real.

It is important to clarify that any generalization such as the military, the police, the government, socialism, capitalism, the poor, the rich, the middle class, and so on, is made full conscious that not all participate in the critique. Human beings generalize for comfort and when they do, do not differentiate between individuals. Generalization is not a good tool in socio-cultural environments, but is the only one we have available to identify offenders. The readers must understand that there are good and bad people in the world and it is impossible to identify them one by one; when we categorize and generalize, we are sinning by exaggeration, but not for omission.

The book has been written in three languages by the author, English, Spanish and French, in that same order, with the purpose of spreading out as soon as possible the precarious and inhuman situation happening in Small Venice. English was the initial choice because it is the most important language in North America. Spanish was the automatic second choice because the story is inspired in a country in South America. Finally, French was the next choice because it is a very important language in North America and the rest of the world. However, the three versions were improved at the same time, they were revised before the final publication that was done in the three languages. A final remark, if it is difficult to write a book in one language, imagine the difficulties making changes to three versions simultaneously.

Introduction

The main character of our story is called Jeremy. He did not plan the undertaken journey a chain of events decided the next step to follow. He was in a Cosmopolitan North American city one day and in a South American town a few days later. He moved from the capital to the town back and forth following his instincts. He was looking for something difficult to find: universal knowledge. He was able to find distorted knowledge instead. The knowledge was distributed among many people and none of them had the complete answer. The knowledge was about politics and society, primarily socialism, a political approach that punishes the individual in favor of the collectivity. Secondly, capitalism is described to contrast with socialism.

The description of Jeremy's journeys during his visits included some dialogues and analysis with educated people in attractive locations of Small Venice. The capital is a cosmopolitan city with over five million inhabitants and Beach Town is located 200 kilometers from the capital and only ten thousands inhabitants. Jeremy is denouncing an accommodating society that allowed the barbarities of Absurd Socialism.

Destiny was his main worry, he lived in a country that could have been like a gold coin but had become a rough stone. The last 18 years have been the worst for the country, improvisers coming from the left took power and destroyed the productive apparatus. Absurd Socialism is a retrograde political form to structure a society that penalizes the members of society and becomes the Dictatorship of the Proletariat. In the world, there are just a few Orthodox Socialists trials going on that are having damaging consequences for the population. Small Venice is the example not to be followed.

In Small Venice the fault cannot be blamed only on socialism, but to the different partners of the regime. It is not convenient to generalize, but they must be identified, the damage is considerable. First of all the military, with the civic military strategy, benefited directly in their own pockets with the wealth that did not go to The People. Besides, they became people's executioners repressing the opponents' manifestations against the government and stayed apathetic during important decision making periods to allow changes in the country. Secondly, many politicians opposed to the regime were permissive, accepting the unacceptable. Many other citizens are to blame for supporting a bad regime, some are just people that do not want to get in trouble or do not care, people that believe it is not their responsibility to play politicians, others do not want to participate in the society, only want to go to work and enjoy life. Finally, there are big and small businessmen that profited the economic disaster using their contacts with the government. The rest are stubborn people that have no better ideas and stay stranded in wrong beliefs.

The regime can be considered the most discriminative government in the modern world. Jeremy is a citizen that has been hurt hard for the Socialist regime that governs the life of about 35 million inhabitants. He knows many cases of discrimination in the country, similar to Germans going after Jewish. Those that opposed the regime had to live with minimum wages because the administrators chased them like dogs with scabies.

He wanted to understand what a society requires; he knows it is a very complex organization and several books are needed to document everything; it would take years of study to define the needs of a society. The technique Jeremy used was basically using dialogues; identify persons with some knowledge, talk to them to find out what was their position on certain social subjects and document his conclusions for human enjoyment. His journeys were useful to clean up the distorted knowledge available.

He also presented his sufferings related to food and medicine scarcity during the last three years of Absurd Socialism wrong policies. It is the first time in more than sixty years that people have suffered such a bad administration of the country; it is the fault of the government. Small Venice is one of the more violent countries in the world, at least 28 thousand violent deaths each year; if in 1987 there were about 3 thousand deaths, the increment up to now is over 900% and the population has not doubled. A violent death does not happen to everyone, but famine is hurting people every day.

His journeys started on issues of society and justice understanding. It is fundamental to understand what a society is, what its characteristics are, what the rights and responsibilities of citizens are. The subject of justice is intimately related with a society, people need opportunities to collaborate in a society. Justice should not be used to mistreat a minority in favor of a majority; the notion of a majority is a political invention with the objective of controlling society and stay in power.

The trip followed with others topics related to politics: democracy, socialism, and capitalism. Democracy is the most pervasive form of government in the world, even Dictators believe in it. With all its defects democracy is the best political approach for administering a society. Socialism and capitalism are two opposing viewpoints that try to get first line attention in the world. Capitalism is an economic approach that has been quite popular whereas socialism is an invention of some proletariat's intellectuals to take power. Capitalism has many defects and needs to reinvent itself. Socialism is flawed, is a failure scientifically demonstrable. The only social aspect of socialism is its name; it is not to help the poor or to improve on justice, it is the opposite.

Some notions about Marxism are presented to point out the real origin of Socialistic ideas. Even though socialist ideas have been around for many centuries, it was the beginnings of Marxism that made socialism popular. Theoretical socialists would need to make a big effort to relaunch socialism, it has been losing popularity for its lack of successful experiences. The worst examples of Absurd Socialism are in effect in some countries and are leaving huge sufferings on the population.

He presented several anecdotes related to personal life experiences and his relationships with family, friends, and acquaintances. He described some idiosyncratic characteristics of people in the country; idiosyncrasy determines why we live such a disaster. Finally, he suffered a series of events that transformed his suffering into a nightmare; a coup d'etat was in effect to change the political structure and bring back democracy to the country. Jeremy felt danger on his entourage and got indirect death threats for his involvement in Political studies. His journey ended badly hurt going back home.

A 'ludic' or gaming approach is presented comparing a game to a society, arguing the pertinence of capitalism instead of socialism. Jeremy paid attention to the activities performed by informal players and their decision-making procedures. With a simple game such as Bingo, where interaction is limited, or a sport such as Soccer, where decisions must be taken in seconds, could establish which were the arguments justifying the experiences and beliefs about what was good or bad practices. For example, how people thought about the organization of the game, how complaints from players were managed, what the idiosyncrasy of the people was, and what values and decision-making processes were utilized.

Talking about games in an analogy to society allows friends and neighbors to participate in simple conversations. Jeremy found a remarkable similarity between what people perceive when they play a game and their beliefs when they support a bad political regime, such as Absurd Socialism. Experiences and comparisons with games contrast model with reality.

Chapter 1: Starting the Journey

Strolling in a known Metropolitan city, Jeremy seemed happy. It was a busy downtown he uses to visit once in a while, primarily during the summer months. He was wondering about his personal problems, his existence, difficulties, life, the society, and politics. Why getting old was going to entail living difficult life experiences, including family and friends' relationships. Why the society he used to live in was deteriorating so fast? Why did a bad government want to stay in power independently of their chaotic administration? What should enlightened citizens do to influence decision makers on the improvement of society?

Today, after living productively for many years, Jeremy had started this journey interested in Society and Games. Games are structured or semi-structured activities usually undertaken for enjoyment purposes, but there are scientific applications of games that are useful. Most games are invented for competitive participation with winners and losers. Some games are educational, guiding behavioral attitudes, and others are just for fun.

People like playing games that involve winners and losers, and we are eternally optimistic that we could be the winners, independently of how badly the odds are stacked against us. There are games used for a purpose, such as simulation, training, analysis or prediction. When Jeremy was studying at the University, he remembers some courses where the subject was the simulation of processes or enterprises in a free market. In one course, the idea was to create groups of students managing their company and competing in a free market. Using some parameters of investment and research, expenses and prices, the simulation produced an overall appraisal and the best company was the winner. At the time there were many other courses that exploited the ideas of modeling and simulation using some type of games.

He continued wondering about the possibility of understanding the disadvantages of socialism using this framework or analogy with a game. He was clear that his proposed approach was not revolutionary; it was just an intellectual exercise that might provide some inside to the problem. It is convenient to clarify that the analogy comparing games with political structures, represents an irony because in reality games do not use to contain political biases.

He wanted to know how people felt about the games, what decisions they took, what importance they showed in some stages, and what criticism and evaluation they manifested at the end. What people do while playing? Who is involved in the decisions? How do they understand the game? How do they organize the game? How do they select their moves? How do they respond to criticism? These were some important considerations.

Games could be used with a purpose, a relationships facilitator, presenting how life and political preferences are interpreted and decided by common people. Using society games, such as Bingo, was an opportunity to observe social interaction. Modeling the society with games could allow him to study some characteristics of people that were attached to the Absurd Socialism regime. A sporting game such as soccer or a board game such as Bingo, could help to demonstrate the inconsistencies of a political strategy such as socialism or capitalism. Showing the advantages and disadvantages of these political strategies applied to a game would clarify some undesirable issues. In principle, a sporting or board game is not associated with politics, but it would be possible to notice how absurd political strategies could be when applied to a game.

Concentrated in his personal and philosophical thoughts, Jeremy was walking into seas of people clustering in the corners to cross the street, when suddenly a friend of him passed by and he recognized his face, "Hello Bertold, How are you doing? I thought you were traveling down South."

"Hi there, I thought you were down South too. Oh well, I have troubles with my knees. After my missed 'Camino of Santiago' walk, I have knee problems and I'll need another operation soon."

"I told you to be careful on that walk in Spain. I suggested you hire a donkey or get a bike for the walk, remember? I was kidding of course, but it was too hard for your legs to walk so many consecutive days at your age, and you already had knee problems at the time." Jeremy remembered.

By the way, Bertold didn't appreciate the suggestion of hiring a donkey, but he recognized that Jeremy was right. At 80 years of age and having knee problems, it was not a good idea to plan for a walk of 20 consecutive days and walking at least 6 hours per day. Bertold had to stop short of his walk after the first four days. He had to flight back home and went to the hospital for knee surgery. Jeremy has known Bertold for over 30 years both are engineers and worked for the same company for many years. They visit the same countries and they get together one or twice a

SOCIALIST BINGO - Germinal Boloix

year. Jeremy has a good appreciation for Bertold, he is a thoughtful and kind personage.

Jeremy wanted to exchange some ideas with him about the problems of societies and asked, "What would you say about an important characteristic of a society?"

His friend reflected for a few minutes and said, "People in a society recognize certain rules of conduct as binding and for the most part act in accordance with them. Remind you that conduct is very important when you live in a just society; without rules of conduct it is impossible to advance."

"But what happens to those that disobey the rules?" asked Jeremy.

"Those that disobey are sidetracked, discriminated. However, Christianity purports well-being for all and claims avoidance of rejection because of wrong behavior. Christians use to give a second chance to those that misbehave."

Jeremy that is not a believer replied, "But some people are mean, they hurt others quite easily, to me they don't deserve empathy."

"Let us give a second chance to all, after that, any penalties would be justified."

People keep cooperating to one another to advance the good of the members of the society, according to Jeremy; cooperation is most of the time welcomed. Cooperation is a form of solidarity, as we wish to interpret it.

His friend demonstrating how deep he thinks about behavior, said, "Not cooperating is different from misbehavior. Penalties related to lack of cooperation should be softer compared with crimes, for example, that are abominable."

Using his recent philosophical advances on society understanding Jeremy added, "Although a society is a cooperative venture for mutual advantage, it is typically marked by conflict. There are interests not necessarily shared by all."

"Many human beings are characterized by egoism and isolation, others want to participate in the community, therefore is difficult to deal with so many different beliefs and personalities."

Jeremy wanted to find out what Bertold thought about justice.

His answer was, "Justice is the legal or philosophical theory by which fairness is administered."

"But, what is fairness? Who decides what is fair and what is not?"

"Justice depends on Culture, therefore on the society we live in." Remarked Bertold.

Jeremy has many simple examples of unjust situations. One is related to the transit of vehicles, one pedestrian crosses the road in a corner with the light in his favor, a car honk its horn and almost hit him turning on the corner; why the driver is so unconscious? Another case is the rule of walking on the right side of corridors or walkways, lots of people do not care for such a simple rule; those people know th rule but they do not follow it for stubbornness; who can do something with that kind of people?

Jeremy was explaining the actual situation of water rationing in Small Venice, imposed by the government; how people suffered every day waiting to fill up the water tanks located on top of the buildings. Those in charge of opening the faucets for the apartments had different criteria, some of them were rational, they knew when water was entering the building and were more flexible with the time. But there was an old lady that was totally inflexible when she was in charge of opening the faucets, she applied just one rule, half an hour exactly, she did not take in consideration if water was entering the building or not; more than once Jeremy was soaked during his shower, he had no time to rinse, the lady had turned off the faucets. The height of the situation came up when they established only 10 minutes of water for the apartments, the old lady argued that because she lived in the top apartments, she was not going to get water so fast, because gravity gave privilege to those living down the building, and that if she did not get water nobody would; luckily nobody listened to her, in ten minutes Jeremy filled up his containers to make his needs. This is a simple example of society mismanagement, people have no brain and apply simple rules to avoid mistakes.

Bertold explained that societies get stuck because people do not obey simple rules. Any policy should be based on human nature; humans do not learn easily, there is no other way. The worst mistake of political systems, socialists, communist, anarchist, is that they do not understand that human beings are defective and too stubborn.

Jeremy's eyes sparked suddenly, he realized the truth expressed by his friend. It was absolutely true, political systems are based on false premises about human beings. Socialism considers humans as beings incapable of progressing by themselves and promotes social help the same to all. Communism considers human beings as perfect, that they behave always well following the rules and they have no ambition. Capitalism on the other side considers everybody saving money, articles, properties, and enjoy life regardless of cost. Anarchism instead considers humans as educated entities that do not need authorities.

Bertold agreed, politicians have not understood human beings. The only parameters handled by socialists are poverty levels and a wrong conception of equality. It is true that capitalism has not solved the problems, but it does not mean that socialism is a solution. Culture is also very important, it has to be well understood in each country context.

"Do you mean that there are many cultures and that societies can have different rules?" Jeremy did exclaim looking a bit confused.

"Of course," Bertold said, "Principles and values are different depending on what religious or ethical principles are followed in each country."

"Would it be possible to affirm that justice is the conception of commonwealth?"

"A society is a collectivity, therefore it is necessary to recognize what belongs to somebody, to establish what is believed to be deserved," completed Bertold.

"Does it mean that a society is constantly supervising citizens and determining what individuals deserve or not?"

"Of course," said Bertold, "It is a way of promoting self-controlling behavior, the society requires some type of regulation to be fair. Justice relates to different concepts found in philosophy, ethics, religion, and law. For example truth, fairness, liberty, fraternity, and equity."

"But listen, in many cases, the rules are not applicable, they depend on the context, let us take the case of a car stop, it should be different during the day compared with the night; it is mandatory to fully stop during the day, but at night the rule should be less strict, no need to fully stop, diminishing only the speed would be enough," said Jeremy, that has been a rebel all his life.

Bertold is less rebel that Jeremy, he has a tendency to be submissive and answered, "I understand your viewpoint, but societies tend to simplify the norms and prefer dismissing the context."

Jeremy was not happy avoiding context and continued, "definitively, a just society must consider the context, there are too many cases where people are punished by this lack of comprehension."

Bertold completed the idea saying that it will take many generations to solve these issues as suggested.

"The notions of justice are primarily in the relationship with other individuals; however, nature and society are impacted by people's decisions," said Jeremy demonstrating his wide knowledge of the universe.

"Today that nature has been hurt by climate changes, it is important to consider the impact of the decisions made by society."

"But," Jeremy said, "Humans live in a delicate environment, any anomalies have repercussions and dangerous consequences."

"Christian principles promote stability, such that the world doesn't get damaged, and consequently human beings remain safe," said Bertold.

Recalling some readings about John Rawls, Jeremy said, "He proposed a model of a just society, defining justice as fairness, establishing the role of justice in social cooperation."

"As you stated, the primary object of justice, according to Rawls, is the basic structure of society: Institutions and the Constitution," said Jeremy that was also influenced by Rawls.

Bertold reflected for a few minutes, there were too many concepts around, "The basic structure of society is related to law and order, therefore it involves the Constitution. Institutions are in charge of controlling compliance with the Constitution."

"Isn't that statement too biased towards the Constitution?"

"I am aware of two or three Constitutions, one of them is relatively short, the American Constitution. The others I know are from South America, and they are way too long."

"Paper admits anything. Not because a Constitution is long, it means is good for the people" said Jeremy recalling Marshall McLuhan expressing the media is the message.

Bertold agreed, "You are right, the Constitution should be written in generic terms to allow flexibility, but it must be precise, to avoid unwanted outcomes. For example, avoid a unique political system running a country indefinitely. Democratic, Capitalistic and Social approaches must be balanced within a society; a good mix makes a difference."

"It would be good to clarify that capitalism is not a political strategy, however, because it holds an opposite view against socialism, it is a good alternative to choose."

"Culture is a key aspect, what are the customs, how transactions are made, how people relate to each other. Cultural changes must be slow, it is not good to precipitate; keep what is good, get rid of what is bad." Jeremy continued.

Bertold explained that justice as fairness generalizes and carries to a higher level of abstraction the traditional conception of the social contract. The social contract was invented many years ago to emphasize the role of the State and limit the freedom of individuals. If laws and institutions are unjust they must be reformed or abolished. Therefore, social contracts must be review periodically.

And added, looking like a professor giving a lecture, "It is the eternal fight between Individuals and States. Those that are benefited by the State try to maintain their advantages. Those that are not benefited are the ones that can start a fight against injustice."

"Rawls said that justice is the first virtue of Social Institutions, as truth is the first virtue of systems of thought" recalled Jeremy.

"In practice, it is almost impossible to be just" reflected Bertold. He kept going saying that there is always somebody against a decision, people are born to complain. The truth is also difficult to generalize everything is not just black and white there are tonalities.

Defiantly, Jeremy said, "According to that, justice and truth are weak concepts. Therefore, it is impossible to get consensus."

"There are so many difficulties in societies, the basics are incoherent."

According to Bertold, justice is a difficult concept, whatever is just to one is unjust to other and people use to have different points of view on the same matters; people analyze things according to their own experiences and understanding. If it is difficult to talk about justice at the society level, imagine how hard it is at the level of small groups, such as a family or small communities. Societies produce written norms, whereas families follow informal norms, each family following its own rules.

"That is the reason why just by going outside on the streets people get in trouble. People around you want to impose their will, according to the way they understand life, most probably different than others," said Jeremy recalling an experience with an 80 years old gang member that banged the car with his fist without justification in the parking lot, because he had stopped too close to him; the old man was saying, "I know the law, I know the law." And Jeremy answered, "You are not teaching me nothing."

According to many, the justice of the poor and socialism is envy, remembered Jeremy. It is clear that when we are born there is some establishment, those that own something want to keep their advantages and those that have nothing want to improve. According to Jeremy, justice is not to take away from the rich to give to the poor, justice must be to give opportunities to the poor to improve by their own effort and live better in the society. Regrettably, poor people believe that if you have something and they do not, then nobody must have it; of course, we mean those people beneath one's dignity.

"People talk about education, the need for everybody to learn and behave in a better way. But what is that way? Who is going to teach you? Has to be the parents? At school?" said Bertold, demonstrating his pedagogical abilities.

Jeremy, that has also been a professor and has had confidence in education for many years, said, "Education has some limits, it is possible to teach techniques and professions, but when we talk about behavior, many people are incapable of learning, they have misbehavior installed inside their genetics."

Bertold that is also up to date on these concepts, agreed with Jeremy and said, "According to recent studies, genetics have a big impact on behavior; we can be born absolutely insensible or exaggerate on sensibility. We are born with virtues and defects."

"Hopefully, over time, people can improve on their defects and adapt to society requirements. But it is a hard job that requires constant learning" said Jeremy doubting of his remark.

"But what is that constant learning? Who is going to teach how to behave? Are parents responsible? At School?" said Bertold demonstrating his research abilities.

"There is too much emphasis on parents, who taught your parents and your grandparents? On the other side, who would teach your children and your grandchildren? Who is going to supervise parents' abilities?" asked Jeremy.

Bertold continued, "According to this, justice, in general, is going to improve slowly. Parents are improvising, most of them have not the required abilities; there is not much improvement to be expected. It will take generations to finally improve on justice."

Jeremy felt depress, he was always interested in education and now he realizes there is no way of educating those born with behavioral problems. "That is the reason some countries do not advance, giving power to individuals with behavioral problems, without sentiments, mistreating everybody around them."

Bertold tried to explain that the situation was not so serious Christians believe that if God wanted things that way, there was a reason. "The world is populated by sons of God, got to be a profound reason to allow that type of leaders; probably it is to give a lesson to us all and forbid the same mistakes."

SOCIALIST BINGO - Germinal Boloix

Jeremy reflected saying that most people do not have time to learn or become intellectuals. Most people are there just for survival, no time for knowledge, no time to read or think, forget about their writing abilities. Others are simply lazy; they don't try to learn or to pursue an intellectual path. Many people spend their time doing no major intellectual effort, only working to make money to live better, and a majority is alive just to survive. Remember that most graduates expect to live the rest of their life without studying again they believe the objective was to get a degree and then earn enough money to live without touching a book or doing research anymore.

The conversation about justice continued for several minutes, Bertold being the most active. He explained that according to Rawls, the notion of justice denies that the loss of freedom for some is made right by a greater good shared by others and freedom is uncompromising. If poor people get an economic benefit, rich and middle class should not lose their autonomy. An injustice is tolerable only when it is necessary to avoid an even greater injustice. In a just society, the liberties of equal citizenship are taken as settled.

"In your next visit to Small Venice," said Jeremy, "don't forget to give me a call. Check first if we are around, it would be a pleasure to have another conversation with you. You have demonstrated how important the notion of justice for human beings is. Survival only is not acceptable for humans; there must be clear approaches on justice for all. Those that love knowledge must have enough time to learn."

Reflecting on the conversation with Bertold, the main subjects were justice, society, human nature and education. A society must recognize its cultural characteristics to define a strategy to improve human prosperity. The issue of understanding human behavior in a society is a key factor in choosing a political strategy. Behavior affects personal relationships to a major degree. In a family, misbehavior causes a breakdown of relationships. In a society misbehavior also destroys the social and human capital.

Chapter 2: Small Venice 'Paradise'

Imagine thousands of kilometers of beautiful beaches, thousands of square kilometers of jungles, hundreds of navigable rivers, hundreds of mountains in the Andes and the North, thousands of square kilometers of prairies, thousands of small towns and hundreds of big cities. Imagine hundreds of thousands of nice people willing to live and let live. Where am I? There must be hundreds of countries that can be described with such words. But Jeremy was thinking about Small Venice, a beautiful country in South America. It is a country with lots of potentials to become rich and prosperous, a country capable of offering lots of opportunities to their citizens. In a word, it is a Paradise.

There are two components that make the difference between paradise and inferno: politics and idiosyncrasy. Depending on the government, a country can develop or not. Small Venice has lots of potential, including human and natural resources, including geographical beauties; additionally, it is one of the biggest oil producing countries and huge quantities of mineral resources are available. How people react to injustice determines the future of a country; the idiosyncrasy of the people makes the difference. In Small Venice, there have been many types of governments: democracies, dictatorships and lately socialism.

Jeremy is a mature man, but he feels quite young. Recently, while he was watching a video of Mick Jagger, he felt singing 'Sympathy for the Devil' on the stage, with lots of hair and lots of energy. Jeremy thought, Why Mick has had at least six wives and is going to be a father at 72 years of age and I have been married just once? I know, I know, he is a multimillionaire. Jeremy is tall, healthy, good looking, bold, and broke; most women would love to hug him and take him for a ride, do not you think? He has had a normal life, passing through all life stages: child, adolescent, young adult, mature adult; at least he knows about most stages of life.

He had the excellent opportunity of having a formal education. He studied at the University and got the highest degrees. He worked as an engineer for many years and specialized later on in computers. He worked in teaching and research most of his productive years. He was always a salaried worker, he was never an entrepreneur. He worked for the University most of the time.

He considers himself an Indigo Child, those children that are born more sensitive and clear minded than most other children on earth. Some

SOCIALIST BINGO - Germinal Boloix

people say Indigo Children are the new stage of human evolution they use to be more empathetic and creative than their peers. There is some kind of instinctive reaction on things that make them unique. Among other things, their intelligence is remarkable. They use to improve anything they do daily, at home, at work, or in the community. Intelligence is the capacity to find improved ways of doing things or reacting instantly and appropriately to an unexpected event.

He recognizes that sometimes his reactions are slow and that he doesn't propose improvements all the time, however, he recalls several successful experiences and some mistakes either. Jeremy thinks that he learns from mistakes, improving on wrong decisions next time he uses that knowledge; including cutting short a friendship if justified, his mental wellbeing is important. In many occasions, he prefers to withdraw, instead of keeping an inadequate relationship.

In 1967, a 6.7 Richter magnitude earthquake hit the capital, while dining with his parents. He was the one who reacted appropriately and took the lead; he stood up and moved out of the dining room to the open corridor. There he waited outside, while his parents followed him not knowing what to do. He remembers the walls at the corridor moving forward and backward, the roaring noise in the background; it was his first experience with an earthquake. It was not his last either.

He is proud of his parents, they were self-educated. They had no chance to go through formal education; they used to read good books and articles and improved their education with experiences in life. His mother spoke the most and told him her anecdotes, while his father was generally silent. His parents helped him to become a successful student and professional, not because of knowing about the subjects, but because they gave him advice about the importance of knowledge. By the way, knowledge is the main ingredient of philosophy.

His parents emigrated from Europe to South America because they were afraid of a third world war. Jeremy was fond of his mother because she demonstrated great knowledge on many subjects, primarily matters of human relationships. Jeremy didn't follow all the recommendations her mother gave him, and in some sense he regrets it. However, he feels that life has been good to him, independently of missed opportunities that defined his path in life.

His parents were humanistic, they called themselves libertarian. They felt empathy toward the anarchy movement in Spain and they participated in the workers' union organization. They never felt empathy towards socialism or communism, though. Jeremy remembers his mother saying about the URRS, "This country plans the life of people since they are born, if they decide you are going to be a laborer, you have no other choice. It is not the individual who decides, it is the government. They do not promote freedom." Jeremy did not appreciate soviets' lack of liberty and was always careful with socialistic ideas.

He comes from a family of workers his father had a small business that barely gave them enough to live. There were no more entrepreneurs close to his entourage. When he was studying at the University, his mother told him, "Keep always present in your mind the working class, they are the ones that struggle the most in life." Jeremy has always had the working class present in his life, and through his supervisory positions, he tried to help them as much as he could. He still wants to help the working class, but he feels that the help is not through the alienation of entrepreneurship or the rich.

He grew up in Small Venice; he arrived when he was a baby. He has many anecdotes from the country, but he would need a whole book to write them up. However, he recalls some of them while being a child. He remembers a friend that lived a few blocks from his home, he does not remember how he met him, was it at school? Or was his mother that knew his parents? Anyway, the name of his friend was Wilson. The house had a big pool and Jeremy was invited many times to plunge for a swim. It seems that Wilson's father was a wealthy businessman during the Dictatorship. Jeremy recalls greatly his friend, but never saw him again.

Being a child, he used to walk around the neighborhood looking for special stones and colorful seeds; some are the very famous black seeds, known as turkey vulture seeds, used to make necklaces. One day walking back home with Wilson, they decided to take a shortcut and passed by through an empty terrain. They found a tall barbed wire fence, his friend was able to crawl over it, while Jeremy almost getting at the top, slept and fell cutting his forehead, he was hanging down from the barbed fence with a wound of more than 10 centimeters. He was lucky not getting stitches, but he was quite impressed by the scar. He still has a visible scar after so many years and sometimes goes and sees how it looks like.

He studied, married, and had children in Small Venice. His wife used to say that he was not a real Small Venice citizen because he was not born there. Jeremy didn't appreciate those remarks because he felt like any other citizen born in the country. Her remarks looked discriminatory; there is no law that can change what you feel. Of course, this type of remarks happen all over the globe where refugees or immigrants set foot; it is the penalty they pay for moving abroad.

Without any specifically planned agenda, Jeremy traveled to North America with his daughters later on in his life. It is possible to say that he was lucky for having that opportunity, the country is one of the best in the world lo live; on the other side Small Venice is living a nightmare. Jeremy uses to travel up and down both countries to visit and is well aware of what is going on.

He started to cook when he was around 40 years old. Before that, he just made some boiled or fried eggs, fried steaks, and spaghetti with butter, cheese, and ketchup. But even though it was a late start, he has been preparing very good recipes the rest of his life. One of his main qualities was that he immediately invented new ways of doing recipes, most of the time getting excellent plates. He made Chinese and Italian plates that everybody enjoyed. The only recipe still giving him some headache is related to the bakery, bread and cakes require precise amounts of ingredients. Jeremy doesn't like so much precision on a recipe, he prefers the touch and feels type of approach.

He still has some relatives in Small Venice and he travels there for vacation purposes. He visits friends and family and goes to the beach to have a good time. In recent years, the economic situation of the country has deteriorated enormously; the Absurd Socialist regime in power during the last 18 years has ruined the country. Small Venice continues fast forward toward its social and economic destruction; the permanence of the socialist regime determines its continuous disastrous future.

He has been writing some books about the problems of life, he spends hours reading and writing about themes related to existentialism. This experience makes him prone to understand many of the difficulties of Live, Love, and Luck. There is a known story, "Love and Interest went to a picnic one day, Interest was the winner and Love was the loser." What Jeremy has learned is that everything is interest, human beings are in the world for interest. People have an interest in breathing, eating, drinking, and any physiological need. Love is another type of interest, whether to love or to be loved; some people may not even have a love interest at all. Economic interest is a particular one people are interested in money to buy things and to live comfortably. Power is another, some want to be close to powerful people, others want to be powerful, and do whatever to stay in power. Justice is another type of interest, people feel the need of imposing justice; their drive is to make justice, to fight for justice, and demand for justice.

Therefore life is interest, no doubt about that. Some interests are innate, some others are acquired, but at the end, everything is interest. It is possible to define priorities related to interest, such as which are healthy and which are unhealthy, but interest is the main driver. Usually, people reject people's money oriented interest, those that have no sentiments and only want economic profit.

According to Jeremy, the main subjects in life and societies are survival, knowledge, and justice. Survival is always present, people are born to survive, there is no other alternative; we must keep breathing, eating, drinking and so on. To survive in a modern society people must work and earn a living, and we must know to survive. Knowledge requires time and effort. People must work hard to learn, life is not an easy task. People must learn to live in any circumstances, knowledge facilitates life. Notions of justice determine the outcomes people choose in their life. The disadvantage with justice is that each individual builds its own notion of justice.

In a society, it is difficult to find people sharing the same principles of justice and there are differences in the way justice is applied. Why is so difficult to find the common patterns of justice that benefit all?

Merit, meaning to deserve something or benefit from something or to be recognized for your accomplishments, should be the driving force that helps to decide what alternative to choose. Some people don't appreciate merit, socialists are an example, they believe in blind equality, where everybody is worth the same, independently of what good or wrong they have done.

Chapter 3: Beach Town Resort

Beach Town is small. Its name comes from the river that runs through it, in the frontier between two important provinces of the country. Sometimes, thinking about Beach Town, Jeremy states, "It is the town that refuses to die." After so many years, the town has not improved as other cities and towns nearby, such as Spirited-Port or Claim-Town. It was founded in the year 1599, but it was not until 1699 that it got the name of Saint John. Beach Town has been around for many years, but progress is not its best adjective, people stay at the same level of poverty for generations. There was a mirage at the beginning of this infamous government, people thought the leader meant what he promised, but sadly they didn't improve because of wrong government policies; today they have realized that they are poorer than before, 18 years have been wasted.

As its name implies, Beach Town, located North-East, has a long, 10 kilometers beach, available for tourism. However, there are not many services available; local governments have not been able to improve on infrastructure. Many houses have been built over the years near the beach, some are in good shape, others are abandoned, and others are invaded by followers of the 'revolution.' From the highway that crosses the town to the beach, there are around 10 to 15 blocks, you can walk from the highway to the beach, it takes about 15 minutes. There is a big stadium near Liberator Square, the most common name used for main squares of towns and cities in the country. it has been there for more than 30 years. Many events are performed in the stadium, including baseball and soccer games. Carnival Parades usually finish their trip at the stadium. Its capacity is about 3000 people.

The population of Beach Town is about 10.000 people. There has been no major increase in the population over the years. Young people tend to move to the capital to continue their studies. The main activities are related to commerce and construction, driven by tourists that own houses or go to all included bed and breakfast lodging. The local government also provides some source of employment, the Municipality is a source of income for local residents, and bureaucracy expands on election times.

There is some small business selling groceries and 'empanadas,' made with corn flour and fillings such as cheese, beef, fish or any other protein mix. There are many liquor stores, they make good business. Lots of people in the town enjoy frenzy drinking during the weekends. There is only one bank, established in the last 5 or 10 years; other services include the electrical and water supply companies. There were two or three Internet providers with seven or eight computers each, today there is none. There are five huge antennas, distributed in the town, for telephone and data transmission, one for each of the companies that provide those services.

The streets are a mixture of gravel, asphalt, concrete or dirt. Every government promises to repair the roads, but few make any big effort to complete the task. Years ago, during the rainy season, cars used to get stuck in the mud and people had to hire trucks' pulling services. There are two or three squares in town besides Liberator Square. The streets are so tough that whatever shoes Jeremy brings in, get worn out fairly fast; most of the shoes he brings in last just a few months. This worn out happens because of the ground, dirt or gravel, and the climate, humid and salted. Years ago Jeremy brought a pair of spare shoes and while walking in a carnival parade, his soles went off and had to throw them in the garbage and kept walking barefoot.

Around 30 years ago, Portuguese immigrants founded small supermarkets in the town, some of them are still alive giving service, but a new wave of Arabs and Chinese immigrants are taking over. Recently, most supermarkets and liquor stores have been founded by Arabs, coming from Syria. Chinese immigrants have taken over most of the grocery stores. Locals still keep their small fisher market or 'empanada' market. There are few restaurants, most of them near the highway and a couple more near the beach resort. There are three bakeries, one close to the highway, and the other two near downtown. Recently, Chinese grocery stores and bakeries were looted and are reluctant to open again.

The Beach Resort has some constructions, a restaurant, bathrooms, and showers. The showers use to be working most of the time, but the bathrooms never work; people maintaining the bathrooms are not used to give good service. In front of the beach, there are palm trees and the restaurant owner rents some tents to protect people from the sun. The beach is acceptable, even though it is not crystal clear; the river brings brown mud and makes the water dirty. During the rainy season, there are lots of branches on the beach because the river brings all that garbage from the mountains. There is a season when it is possible to catch clams on the shore, they are called 'Guacucos', and people tend to get as much as they can to make 'empanadas de Guacuco.'

SOCIALIST BINGO - Germinal Boloix

The weather in Beach Town, during July and August, is brutal, the temperature raises over 40 degrees centigrade and the sun is inclement. It is possible to state that people in Beach Town are suffering from hot weather mania; it is difficult to work with so high temperatures. It is remarkable that construction jobs are still done on those conditions, workers can be congratulated for such an effort. It is understandable that in some periods of the year there are no workers available.

One special characteristic of the people in Beach Town is that they are friendly. Some of them are very interested in getting an economic or service benefit from their friends and from the municipality. When people have to strive hard to survive, know that it's better not to get in trouble with neighbors; help may be needed sometime in the future. According to philosophers, friends feel good getting together and enjoying a conversation without any attachment to possible favors. However, when people live for survival, they need to maintain relationships for the sole purpose of assuring a future favor.

Most people in Beach Town have always been associated with some political party, primarily the one in power. People use to believe that each government is in charge of helping them and they ask for favors as much as they can. They are used to ask the local government for work, subsidies, appliances, construction materials, and even homes. Some governments have given money and gifts, but as we all know, it is impossible to satisfy the needs of everybody. Lately, food and medicines are the most requested supplies in town. Needs have been turning to basics, survival is more important than work or family. People do need help, and the government is incapable of solving the basic problems, what can you expect from a bad government? Nothing!

Locals maintain a relationship with tourists because they foresee the possibility of having some kind of economic benefit. In the same way that somebody keeps acquaintances for economic reasons, locals have an economic interest in the relationship with tourists. The relationship of locals and the political party in power is because of the economic benefits they may get. Economic interest is not new; it has been around for many years since democracy started. To exploit that weakness, the leader of the revolution knew how easy it was to have people loyal to his regime, just give some income or benefit and they will sell their soul.

A neighbor accepted the construction of a barn on her property for purposes of growing fighting cocks; the last Mayor was a fanatic of cockfights and he proposed to build a barn to grow cocks. Fanatics of fighting cocks helped the Mayor to convince the lady to allow the construction of the barn. In exchange, the lady gets some consideration from the leaders of the municipality and favors from the party in power. Cocks use to start singing quite early in the morning, those that live close to the barn have to get used to that music of the birds and get up early.

Some neighbors have been able to get houses from the government; nobody knows whether they pay their debt or not, but they live in those 'free' houses happily. Some neighbors are ultra-fanatic of the government, they even talk well about the revolution; they are unable to recognize that there is no revolution at all, everything was a mirage. According to Jeremy, people do not believe in any revolution and that is an advantage, anytime the regime can be changed without a major confrontation.

People has no consideration for ideology, all is simple economic interest. They have no time to read about what socialism means, therefore everything is economically biased. Those that keep some type of ideological view, support the government because they believe the collective must crush the individual. This type of viewpoint is supported by people that have never lived well enough they think that socialism is an alternative, different from capitalism, to improve their lives. On their own they will never improve, usually, they have no education or profession to earn their lives by themselves.

The house where Jeremy stays is around three blocks from Liberator Square, it requires time-sharing; other family members may be planning to visit anytime. The house is also known as the house that refuses to die, the same as the town. Asphalt, in front of the house, just happens to be done recently; it was a gravel street all these years. It was first owned by an economy professor forty years ago, it is made with concrete blocks and asbestos roof. Initially, it was 60 square meters, today is 120 square meters; it is very modest, with two bathrooms and two bedrooms, everything is rustic. At the beginning, 35 years ago, there were only two houses in the neighborhood, built by the same constructor. Today, only one house, in front, has not been finished, it was started about ten years ago and the owner never completed his mission.

The main problem of the house came about 20 years ago when the municipality decided to build the streets, surprise! The house was suddenly below street level. The gap was close to one meter; the problem was solved by lifting the floor level, but the roof is low now, it requires to be lifted up at least a meter. Besides repairing the floor inside the house, and pouring one meter of dirt and concrete on the floor, it required pouring lots of dirt around the house to avoid water condensation during the rainy season. The house had a dozen palm trees, planted thirty years ago, but today only three are left; there is an insect that kills the plant by entering the branch at the top of the tree. The climate and the dirt are so harsh that no tree stands so terrible conditions; many trials were done to plant mango or little cherries; it does not matter what kind of tree, they don't progress and die, the only tree that can succeed is a palm tree.

Currently, there is no refrigerator or air conditioner; the reason is that vandalism is always storming the house and being a vacation spot, it is better not to risk other assaults. There are a small gas stove and a gas container, but because of gas scarcity, it is not possible to cook. The government controls the main gas distribution system, it has been impossible to find a container, provided by the government, and impossible to replenish the existing gas container, because the company is not working in the area anymore; this is one more of the thousands of companies bankrupted by the socialist government. There are an electric stove and a small electric oven to help cook simple foods. There is one bed, difficult to move to avoid robbers, a couple of hammocks, a few chairs, one table, and a couple of fans.

At beach Town, Jeremy's experiences relate to his own family and some close neighbors. His relatives live in North America and Europe, only memories are kept when the wind blows. Many years ago when Jeremy used to go to Beach Town with his family, he used to go in the morning to the beach, coming back to the house in the afternoon. After getting a shower, he used to go buy some groceries or grab something to eat at the local 'empanada' houses. At night Jeremy used to watch TV or talk to neighbors if there were not exams to be marked. For many years he repeated the same routine, he visited some neighbors and others came to visit him and his family, some were friendly than others of course.

Marbella is the lady that takes care of the house in town lives just behind it, crossing the street to the left. She is over fifty years old, she was taking care of her grandson for many years, but now he left to pursue his studies at the capital. Marbella has other grandchildren and uses to take care of them during the day. She also helps her sister, taking care of a four years old kid. She is not working, but she makes ice cream for the neighbors. She got some loans from the government to make ice cream many years ago. She sells the ice cream to the neighboring kids that pass by, there is an ad in front of her house, written in a cardboard by hand, 'Ice cream for sale, mango, lemon, chocolate, 300 Pesos each.'

She has some influence in the community and has been close to the municipality; lately, she has been in charge of distributing food to the community. The Socialist government wants to impose their monopoly on food distribution. The municipality uses to prepare a list of neighbors that can receive food at regulated prices. Marbella is in charge of receiving the packages and distribute them. Jeremy was surprised not getting one regulated package because he is a tourist, he thinks it is discrimination. Why is he not going to get one package of food at lower prices while he is in town?

The mother of Marbella also lives close by. Jeremy has known her for many years she used to take care of his palm trees. She is a lady that has worked all her life and never got a benefit from a government. Today she still is pro the deceased leader of the revolution because she thinks this government made some contribution to improving on poverty and she got her age security pension. Sometimes, she had expressed that justice has been done, "now everybody is at the same level of poverty, the medium class is having more difficulties than before and the poor class is having less difficulties." She said that three years ago, for sure she is suffering a lot today when the income is not enough to buy food.

She is not so happy with the looting going on now, but it is possible to think that she is not against the regime; it is a case of exaggerated stubbornness. He believes that what you get when you age is well deserved, it is because of you and not the government; staying alive in this country, with so much crime, is enough of a struggle.

Jeremy and his family used to talk to a neighbor close by, Minerva, she works for the local administration. She lives full time in Beach Town her house is located close to Jeremy's, just crossing the street. Minerva was born in Beach Town but she moved to her house about fifteen years ago when she got married with another local of Beach Town. She had already two children when she married and she had three more children with her new partner. Jeremy has known these kids for many years since they were born. They used to come to the house and sit on the porch. She has been divorced for at least five years now, but both partners still live under the same roof, in different rooms. Do you imagine living under the same roof with your ex-husband? It seems this happens in the world more than you can imagine.

While her kids were small, they used to visit Jeremy on weekends and spent some time talking about common daily life events, now they are grown up, they don't visit anymore. Jeremy had the opportunity to know how smart these kids were. Two of them were outstanding, in the good sense of the adjective, had good answers to common situations that demonstrated how well they would be doing in life. Other didn't demonstrate so much capacity, some were relatively lazy, they didn't try hard on whatever they did, maybe their life would be harder, who knows. Jeremy remembers telling one of them, "Listen, why don't you see yourself in a mirror? Your behavior is getting a little bit too obsessive." He meant that she needed to behave.

Playing marbles with one of her sons two or three times was a memorable experience. They draw a triangle on the dirt and put inside several marbles, the idea was to get marbles out of the triangle shooting with your own marble from the outside; if the opponent hit your own marble he won all the marbles inside. The other game was opening small holes in the ground, around four, separated by a meter, and making a tour of marbles, passing by all the holes; shouldn't let your opponent hit your own marble; the one completing the tour first would win a certain amount of marbles.

Minerva's ex-husband is the typical man of Small Venice, smart, autonomous and macho. He made his life traveling and living up and down the country. Ten years ago he had a job at the municipality that he kept for a few years. At the time, he didn't complain much about the government, but after been laid off, he started to talk back against the socialist regime, as many others suffering discrimination. Lately, he has found another job helping in a Bed and Breakfast lodge and also has worked in construction. He has been related to political opposition parties, helping those organizations during election times. His idea, of course, is to get some influence in the event of a change of government. When the couple started to have matrimonial differences, Jeremy was in favor of Minerva, he hated macho positions; he couldn't approve her ex-husband wrong doing.

Independently of the couple's problems, Jeremy has some anecdotes involving her ex-husband. First of all, he is a melomaniac, he has an extensive music library and he uses to play it aloud as much as he can; he has huge speakers that sound kilometers around. When Jeremy told him he was a melomaniac, he said, "Be careful with what you say, I do not like to be insulted. Why are you calling me that? What do you mean? Are you out of your mind?" He demonstrated macho ignorance.

The other anecdote about her ex-husband is related to the common hobby of drinking liquor. Drinking liquor is the worst distraction in the country. Every weekend, people, mostly men, get together to drink beer and liquor all night. In Beach Town, men get in front of liquor stores and spend hours drinking and talking. Jeremy uses to stop at the liquor store but to buy water bottles instead of liquor, people watch him with suspicion, "Why this guy is buying water instead of a refreshing beer or some booze?" Jeremy saw several cases of fights, pushing and falling. Once, a drunk man felt after being punched, he crashed his head on the floor, the sound was like a coconut, without skin, thrown on the ground; Jeremy still remembers today the cracking sound. After a few beers, it is easy to get into a fight for any reason, alcohol is not a friend of anyone it stimulates violence.

A long time ago, when Jeremy dropped off by the ex-husband's house, he offered Jeremy some liquor, "Whiskey or beer, your call." Jeremy drank a glass sometimes, but most of the time he refused the offer.

Not getting into the drinking tradition makes Jeremy quite happy. He has felt the effects of alcohol only a few times in his life. The first time, when he was young, working during summer in an urban construction site as an assistant topographer, placing the rule, for Theodolite measurement of the terrain. One Saturday at noon, after getting the paycheck, he went with his peers to a house where whiskey was sold, he drank close to half a bottle; he doesn't know how he got home. He took the bus and ride around the city for a few hours, he had difficulty finding the right stop near his house, couldn't open his eyes widely. Jeremy remembers getting home around five or six o'clock and went directly to bed, his mom saw him and understood that he was drunk. Jeremy slept till next morning.

At the ex-husband's house, Jeremy was talking about the political situation and from nowhere, the ex-husband said, "Listen, I don't trust you at all, you use to refuse liquor when I offer some, you are distrustful. It is very strange for me to know somebody that doesn't drink much. I am used to drinking lots every weekend and you drink nothing."

Trying to find some excuse, Jeremy said, "What happen is that I take some pills and it is not convenient for me to drink liquor at the same time."

The ex-husband's responded, "I see, but still, you refuse more than accept. It is not normal behavior in this country, maybe you are hiding something, are you a spy?"

"If I were getting a salary for not drinking it would be nice to keep doing it forever. If you know somebody paying to be a non-drinking spy, put me on the list, volunteer." Jeremy continued, "By the way, are you hiding something yourself?"

SOCIALIST BINGO - Germinal Boloix

"These days thing are getting ugly, the regime is supported by the Island, and you know how difficult it is for dissidents to live in the Island. It may happen also in our country; spies are getting information and sending it to the Island Intelligence Agency that controls our life."

He didn't continue talking about the subject, didn't find it amusing and liquor was having an effect on the ex-husband's conversation.

In town there are many ladies with difficulties raising their kids; most are single mothers and lacked the education to help their kids. It was clear in many cases that the kids were problematic. One of those girls got noticed everywhere she went; it is unclear if it was a matter of personality, behavioral difficulties, desire to show off, or mental illness; she was always bothering in one way or another. Her mother was unable to improve on her behavior, the lady was not educated enough to help her daughter and had no place to find assistance, the country has no good Institutions to help in those cases. She was known as a spirited child because of her stubborn character; it is only what she says that counts, others have no opinion.

One thing was evident, she had difficulties obeying and always wanted to do her way; in several occasions she confronted her mother over her chores, getting into arguments or disobeying. She did what she pleased most of the time. It is a shame having children like that, people around tend to point to the parents for not educating their children. What those people don't understand is how difficult it is to raise these kids.

A neighbor was asked to become her godmother, Jeremy told her not to accept that responsibility because everybody knew how often she misbehaved and the future implications of being a godmother. Not paying attention to the suggestions, the lady accepted the responsibility and became her godmother; that decision allowed her to know the girl more closely and she had an informed opinion about her behavior. She knows how economically interested she was; wants expensive gifts and lots of consideration and empathy.

At eleven years old, she started to have boyfriends at school that lasted a few months at a time. She didn't like to help her mother, didn't clean or cook; she was lazy, only stayed outside with friends. She tended to get into arguments with her mother or at school, most of the time she shouted at people that didn't comply with her. Sometimes, when she got home late and her mother complained, the girl started talking back or having an attitude. The neighborhood got aware of their loud fights.

When she was 13 years old, she began to have a more serious relationship with a mature male teenager of about 18 years old. So she decided to start up this relationship and she left her home to go live with him at the boyfriend mother's place. Her mother did not agree with this decision but at the end, after some arguments, she let her daughter leave home.

When a girl misbehaves as she did since being an infant, and gets not enough advice, it is almost impossible to recover. Her mother was the main responsible for her fate, however, the only way to prevent this behavior is to act on time, and give good advice while there is still a chance of improvement. If her mother had had the possibility of counseling and advice, receiving help on how to be a parent of a difficult child, things might have been different.

Parents must be more decisive on these situations because letting children do whatever they want is harming their future. It is a never ending story, the kids repeating more or less the same life their parents followed, a life of irresponsibility.

Many people in town didn't follow a formal education, went to primary and secondary school but did not graduate. They have no profession, and no particular skills to make a living. Their case is common in the country, persons that don't work most of their life, or that work very informally. They get some income here and there, but they don't pay rent and most of the time, don't even pay for food or clothing. It is a pandemic, lots of people live in those conditions, without producing any benefit or income, it is a shame.

There is the case of a neighbor, over 60 years old, that was caught transporting drugs in an airport; it is serving a 15 years sentence given by the society. He was spoiled primarily by his sisters; he rarely held a permanent job. It is strange that he lingered for so many years without misdeed. The man had no need to get into drug trafficking, it is the fault of the family because they supported laziness all his life.

This type of situation is quite common in the country. Males or females that live close by their family and because they do not like to work, stay with them for long periods of time. It is a cultural custom that should be dealt with. It is OK to help an adult for some time, but not for life. These people live like rich, being poor, they have no responsibilities, they do not help at home, they get bed and breakfast, they even ask for money from others, those that do the sacrifices.

SOCIALIST BINGO - Germinal Boloix

Summarizing the cultural or idiosyncratic characteristics highlights, some positive aspects are:
- People have a good sense of humor despite the bad situation
- There are good workers and some hard workers; climate has a negative effect on productivity
- People are basically tolerant
- They are good people, even though I am in my house and you are in yours
- They use to live and let live
- Children criminality in town is low compared to the rest of the country

Some negative aspects are:
- As well as in the rest of the country, there is machismo, not only in the dominant behavior toward women, but also in confrontational and authoritarian dealing with others
- There are too many cases of divorce or separation letting children primarily on the hands of mothers; they have to do huge sacrifices to raise their kids; it is a matter of father's irresponsibility
- A drinking habit affecting mostly men and damaging the family
- Many cases of early adolescent pregnancy
- Some cases of extreme children's disobedience
- Many cases of adult relatives living with their families because they do not take responsibility for their lives. These people live like rich, being poor, that is so good!

Chapter 4: Traveling to Beach Town

When Jeremy visits Small Venice, he stays in a small apartment located in downtown, on the Center-East side of the capital. He is lucky to have a place to stay during his vacations; it is difficult to find lodging on turbulent times. Apartments are hard to find, there is not much offer around; owners do not appreciate the renting policies imposed by the government; owners prefer to have an empty apartment; the government has suggested many times the possibility of invading apartments. There are hundreds of building invaded by loyal supporters of the regime.

The location, in a busy neighborhood, makes the apartment full of dirt in a few days. With the windows closed, the dirt remains outside, but once the windows are opened, dirt starts to accumulate; the traffic is heavy during busy hours, the smoke of exhausts makes it difficult to breathe. Jeremy has to wipe floors every two days, there is charcoal powder all around; pollution is remarkable. Jeremy is not sure how bad it is for his lungs, but he is always worried about his health, he has known more than one dying of lung cancer; when he is in the apartment, uses to have colds and sore throats.

When he travels from the capital to Beach Town, he uses to get up around five in the morning. It is early and dark, but in half an hour, sunlight starts to clear up his vision. He gets his bag ready the night before: some sheets for the bed, a few shirts, depending on how many days he stays, a couple of socks, a short, a swimming suit and some few tools in case he has to do some repair while at the house in the town; he has to bring also some soap, toilet paper, and deodorant to fight scarcity of resources in the country. He has to do a few things before leaving, for example, get a short bath, if there is running water available. He prepares a snack for the trip and follows the ritual of turning off some appliances, the gas supply, and the water main key, closing the windows, and turning off fans and lights. A note with instructions is on the door such that nothing is forgotten.

It was a day in March for the trip. He had a pretty bad cold with lots of nasal congestion. He didn't understand why a cold affects him so much, it starts with a running nose that last a few days, then follows with some cough, and finally the cold disappear; the cold uses to lasts three or four weeks. Last time it was pretty serious, it lasted at least three months with a strong cough. In recent years people's health has been menaced by the lack of food and medicines. There are many cases of virus affecting the

SOCIALIST BINGO - Germinal Boloix

population and the government is incapable of solving the issues. It is incredible that there is not yet a revolt in the country, the government is doing nothing to improve the conditions.

Walks from the building to the subway station, it takes him less than ten minutes. There is not much traffic at that time, just a few buses that make loud noises with their exhausts and horns. The streets look mostly dark, brown colors most of all and the buildings are Grey, it is not a nice picture. The metro starts to work at five thirty in the morning, but he prefers to arrive later such that he doesn't need to wait outside while the doors open, insecurity is always a concern even early in the morning. There are 8 stations from the start to downtown, near the bus terminal. When he gets to the last stop, he walks to the terminal, it takes about ten minutes to arrive.

Early morning, close to the terminal, the streets are usually full of people, some of them are preparing their items for sale on the floor; the stairs and floors look abandoned, many years without maintenance and it is dirty, getting a bit repugnant. He arrives at the bus terminal around 6:30 am. He uses to take the same route through the parked buses to get to the one that goes to Beach Town. He has had no problems up to now, but he has heard of many cases of pocket lifting and he prefers to avoid that. Insecurity is always in the air, increased poverty affects crime.

When he arrived at the bus stop saw his neighbor Charlie on the line, he was traveling that day too. There were two or three more people behind him and he was talking with somebody else.

"Hello Charlie, I know where you are going," said Jeremy.

"Hi there, yes, of course, you guessed right, we know where we both are going. Listen, if you get on the bus before me, please keep me a spot beside you".

Jeremy didn't know why he said that, because Charlie was first on the line, and said anyway, "Don't worry, I'll do it."

Charlie has been traveling to Beach Town for many years, probably more than 40. He has been used to the buses much more than Jeremy has. While at the bus line, Jeremy asked the driver how much the fare to Beach Town was.

The driver replied, "This bus is going to cities located further than Beach Town, and we charge 800 Pesos."

"Wouldn't it be cheaper for us going to Beach Town?"

"If you stop at Beach Town you must pay the same fare" according to the driver.

Charlie was not happy to pay an extra 200 Pesos to travel. Jeremy told him that it was better to pay the 800 Pesos and travel early in the morning than wait until noon for the next bus going direct.

And complained to the driver, "But the fare to Beach Town is cheaper than that, why don't you charge less?"

The driver was not happy to yield, but after going up and down the allies, he came back and said: "Ok, pay the regular fare to Beach Town."

The normal fare is 600 Pesos. The drivers try to charge more, saying that they are supposed to go far to other cities where the fare is more expensive and that they lose some money accepting passengers that drop before the final destination. Jeremy understood it is a way of getting more income, charging the full fare to everybody. These years have been inflationary, last year it was around 200%, this year is expected to be around 700% and next year could be 800%; he was not kidding, inflation is huge, misery is growing, we are all going to be skinny even if we do not want to. Add the shortage of food, medicines, and hygiene supplies and the expectation is dramatic; it is possible to say that life expectancy has diminished at least five years because of so many difficulties. According to international studies, life expectancy would diminish to about fifteen years in the years to follow.

They finally got into the bus, Jeremy found two places and he sat beside Charlie. They were talking about the economic situation in the country, why there are so many people making lines to buy regulated products such as corn flour, butter, sugar, oil, rice, toilet paper, soap; people were lucky to find chicken, beef, and fish, even though the prices were quite high.

"I feel bad for those people in lines, complaining about their anguish. I listen to what they say, many of them are getting mad, some start early at 4 or 5 in the morning, sometimes they are sick or they need to take care of some family member," said Charlie looking worried and sad.

"To me, being aware of the lines is enough of a reason to understand that there is a severe problem in the country; I don't need to listen to what people say in the lines, I know they are complaining. I complain myself, just because I see them, and I normally don't want to get into a line. The government has been incapable of solving such a relatively simple matter: provide enough food for all. It was the fault of the government not paying supplier's debts. The government wanted to be smarter than everybody else, saving some money and affecting entrepreneurs. The lines started over three years ago now, and they are getting worse day after day." Jeremy said, demonstrating his understanding of justice.

SOCIALIST BINGO - Germinal Boloix

Lines were primarily the fault of the government, no doubt about that. The last 60 or more years did not acknowledge a similar scarcity situation. However, there is a psychological component that must be recognized. Many people do get supplies and food over time; those that keep track on a timely basis of what products are available. They buy the maximum amount of food or supplies allowed by the government and they have reserves at home. Psychologically, people buy much more than needed when the government puts limits it is a natural human reaction. Those that suffer the most are people that had no time to stay on a line or people that travel once in a while to the country as Jeremy did. That is the reason why there has not yet been a social commotion, a majority still finds something to eat.

The regime, calling themselves Socialists of the Twenty-First Century has been systematically dominating all the Institutions, getting rid of entrepreneurs by not paying its debts, confiscating farms and industries, and worst of all, applying harsh money exchange rate controls that have put imports under a paralysis. During the 18 years of this bad regime, more than one hundred fifty thousand companies have gone bankrupt. Add to that the famous Discriminating List, affecting millions of people because of signing against the infamous leader of the revolution; if you signed against the leader, you put your job in jeopardy, losing it or getting discriminated, or downsizing to part time jobs instead of keeping your full-time job. The regime had a systematic policy of punishing the opposition. Public administrators applied a miserable persecution to people that did not agree with the regime. Even today, when people are requesting the resignation of the President, there are government officials menacing those signing of losing their jobs.

The bus started to move through the city, traffic was relatively heavy but much better than other times. Jeremy remembered when he was caught in traffic once, and nobody moved in the highway for hours. Now, because of his cold and congestion, he had no desire to talk much, luckily there was another passenger, also going to the town, sitting just beside Charlie that made most of the talking. Jeremy preferred to close his eyes and rest a bit because he felt tired. The conversation was centered mostly toward the country's bad economic situation.

Passengers were talking about the daily difficulties, "Have you heard any explanation from the government on how the country income has been distributed? Was the leader of the revolution accountable? Was the extra income for oil high prices ever declared? Where did the extra money go?

Why did people not complain about that? Why nobody seems to care?" Everybody agreed this was a regime that was not accountable and people accepted it comfortably.

"This is a government that wants to follow Marxism, without knowing anything about it. By the way who has ever understood what Marx wrote? I started to read the Capital and I could not pass Chapter 12, the book is unreadable" said Jeremy showing off his latest readings about Marxism.

Their faces of passengers demonstrated that they didn't know much about Marxism or socialism. People don't care about ideology, they only care for the daily livelihood, get enough to eat and provide to your family; most people are at the lower level of Maslow's Hierarchy, satisfying survival needs only.

The trip took three hours, and there was no disturbance or noise during the trip, the bus was one of those few that did not play loud music. 90 percent of the time, the buses use to play popular music during the full trip. They play salsa, rumba and 'bachata' aloud, never classical music. We were relatively lucky this time, no loud music at all! Independently of the noise, people use to sleep and chat with their neighbors.

The bus arrived in town at noon, the sun was strong and it was humid, they walked from the bus stop toward their houses and passed by the small market fair. Charlie stopped at the market and bought some 'cassava.' It is made with tapioca starch and is considered a healthy carbohydrate. Jeremy decided to buy some too, he paid 300 Pesos for five cakes; prices are changing day by day; a couple of weeks before paid for the same cakes 200 Pesos. The prices are going up at least 100% every month, how much would cost five cakes, two or three weeks later, maybe 500 Pesos or more. The prices were going crazy lately; the inflation rate during the last year was the highest in the hemisphere. The country has the higher misery and inflation rate in the world. If prices keep escalating, there is going to be a social explosion, nobody stands this.

"People use to stand worse situations, take the case of the Island, where people have been going on for a similar scarcity and after more than 50 years they still stand the Castro's family in power," said Jeremy demonstrating a deep understanding of the Island difficulties.

"Yes, but I remind you that our country is not the Island, we have gone through social explosions before, and they brought changes of government," said Charlie, maybe remembering the time when the Fat Dictator was ejected in Small Venice.

SOCIALIST BINGO - Germinal Boloix

"Yes, I know, but this regime has been in power for 18 years now and it is still there, everybody knows that socialistic regimes are not capable of improving the living conditions for the people, they use to worsen their livelihood," said Jeremy signaling socialism defects.

Because of oil high prices, people got used to living easily, without doing much, receiving aid from the government. The problem is that now, the prices are low and the government has no money to give away. Most people don't care about the political system, provided they get a share of the country's wealth.

"You are right, most people don't care about politics, they care only about survival," said Charlie.

Charlie had a house just 50 yards from Jeremy. He sold it and moved, around five years ago, to another house a block farther, closer to the beach. Charlie used to work as a clerk for many years in a government warehouse, he managed the inventory. He has been married for many years, his wife was a teacher and she is retired. He has three daughters and five grandchildren; they use to visit him during vacations. His hobby is fixing his house, spends hours and hours doing something in the house, new rooms, new doors, new floors, new walls. Sometimes, he hires a worker, other times he does things himself.

Many years ago, when Jeremy went to Beach Town on weekends, usually Friday afternoon, he was tired. Charlie used to arrive late on Friday night or Saturday morning, and the first thing he did was to play his loud music for several hours until late night. Fridays, Jeremy had trouble to sleep with such a noise. Jeremy was not happy with that music so late, at the time, Jeremy was a professor and he used to bring some work to be completed during the weekend. Jeremy needed some rest every night to be able to carry on his task; he worked mostly during the day, reviewing essays, programs, correcting exams, or preparing material for the classes. Charlie's music got Jeremy acquainted with popular songs, such as salsa, cha-cha-cha, rumba, son, and boleros. Later on, he became a bit of a fan of that music and he bought some records himself; her daughters also became fans of that music too. It meant that an unwanted loud music became a nice hobby later, listening to Latino music.

Charlie and Jeremy kept talking while walking toward the houses, at the corner, they said, "Ok, see you later, I have to solve some problems at the house, it seems there is no electricity."

"Ok, see you later."

Arriving at the house Jeremy had to define what was happening with the electricity, why there was no light in the house. When he got close to the electricity pole, one cable was cut off hanging half way on the other side; somebody had stolen a long piece of cable, about 10 meters long. Somebody climbed on the pole and cut off one cable, they went down at the other side of the street and cut the piece off; it was not easy to see the cable missing because there still was a branch of cable in place.

He talked to his neighbor Marbella that takes care of the house. "Marbella, I found out what happened, somebody cut off one branch of the cable."

"Oh, I did not realize the cable was cut off, I have some extra meters of cable, if you need. I can sell you some; find somebody to install the cable. The cost of cable today is about 1000 Pesos per meter at the hardware store. I am going to give you a better price, don't worry too much."

"It is OK, I'll pay for whatever it costs, is there somebody you know to connect the cable?"

She said that there was somebody around and that she was going to contact him. In the afternoon, around 5 pm, the guy came by and fixed the cable.

He paid Marbella 6000 Pesos for the 10 meters of cable and he gave the guy a 2000 Pesos payment for the job. He was happy to have some electricity for the night, to be able to run the fan and sleep cool.

Chapter 5: Democracy at Pleasure Valley

Politically, Jeremy has always been a liberal. He had intellectual ties with the left most of his life, but did not become a permanent activist. However, the last eighteen years represent his real contact with a regime calling itself Socialist. When Jeremy was young, influenced by his parents, he had some attachment with anarchism. He always felt that the individual was the most important participant in society and that educated human beings don't need a government. Military and policemen are unwelcome, they represent authority by force. Many years of experience make Jeremy understand that some kind of government is necessary and human beings have too many defects that require 'convincing strategies.' Governments should be quite different from what we got now and he stills believes strongly on the individual. When the individual behaves, there is no real need for an imposed authority.

Instead, he fears collectives their behavior is random and destructive; people don't take good decisions when masses are in charge. He would never put the collective interest above the individual; there is always the possibility to group individuals according to their specifics, different from a global collective Utopian need.

Why, 2500 years ago, thought Jeremy, Greek philosophers speculated about well-administered societies, those that made the citizen prosperous. Those philosophers were the only ones that thought about life and its difficulties. They suggested that a society is a more or less self-sufficient association of people sharing similar life objectives, where merit was one of its biggest assets. Greeks lived in a society where knowledge was pretty much important, and some citizens expended most of their time arguing about ethical issues. Most Greeks were wealthy, that allowed them time to think. However, their society was not perfect, they had slaves as servants. Independently of this injustice, Greeks were remarkable in their search for knowledge.

"Why modern societies are not so interested in knowledge as ancient societies were?" thought Jeremy. He still remembers a conversation with an old man that used to cut the grass in his house. The old man was having lunch in the porch and suddenly told Jeremy, "there is no need to know too much, people only need the day to day knowledge to survive." Jeremy was astonished, an old man that maybe has never gone to school saying that people do not need to go find knowledge. He was a bit disturbed, always looking for knowledge and now an old man telling him that. The only explanation was that the old man did not need much knowledge during his life, he was satisfied with what he got and did not want to spend more time; he was not curious. Jeremy forgot to ask if the old man knew how to read.

Knowledge has to do with understanding, intelligence and natural reasoning. Every human being knows something, knows how to do something, understands something. What is important is to do things better, let us take the example of boiling eggs, everybody knows how to do it, but it does not mean that we cannot do it better. Most people use a watch to count how many minutes boiling, three minutes, five minutes, more minutes, an so on. There is a way of boiling them without a watch. Place the eggs into a cooking pot with cold water, place it on the hot top of the stove and wait until it starts boiling strongly, turn off the stove and wait a few minutes until it gets colder. The eggs are going to be always the same, a yellow orange color, never gray. This new way of boiling eggs represents a new knowledge embodied in life.

It is important not to confuse knowledge with beliefs or opinions. Beliefs are the fact of believing in something that may be apparently or possibly true, but we have no certainty. People that believe in God have the beliefs but they have no certainty. Jeremy remembers when he was a child, he had never gone in front of the sea and he heard the news that a young mas was dragged by a wave; inside his head the wave, his belief, was a big bubble where the young man was glued and was taken away from the shore. On the other side, an opinion is an attitude expressing something we believe possibly true, but that we have no certainty either. People love to give opinions, push imagination to possible scenarios of what can be true.

Knowledge has also a component that is usually forgotten most of the time: get some knowledge requires effort. Many people express they know a language without taking enough time to master it. They say they know the language, but if somebody rebukes them, they show their ignorance. To learn a language well you need, on average, 7 years living in an environment to practice the language doing oral exercises, writing and reading. Additionally, it is clear that we need all our life to learn our mother language, there is always something new to learn, therefore to learn a new language requires at least the same time.

Jeremy remembers one event trying to teach how to make white rice to a family member without using a watch. He was explaining, but the family members did not pay attention, they were not interested in learning, they did not care, they had some other problems that were more important to them. If the one expected to learn does not makes an effort, time is lost.

He remembers when he was a teenager, his father bought him a musical instrument, a kind of guitar with four strings, called 'Four,' that is typical in Small Venice. Jeremy got the Four and a brochure, he remembers trying to play, but he was never capable of producing a significant sound. He had to wait until maturity to have the opportunity to take some classes and learn a few songs; it was his own effort that allowed him to learn, as well as the help of some instructors. He uses to play once a year when he gets the chance to find a Four and a brochure.

He decided to visit an old University, where he used to teach several years ago, to find out some answers. He knows many Professors, some are nice others do not. Jeremy knows that in many Universities around the world, some Professors believe they are saviors overqualified. Those are the ones that want to maintain their old viewpoints, not allowing innovation and variety; for example, pure math is a different career than computer science, therefore should allow engineers, architects or other types of professionals to enrich the knowledge base. Jeremy knew several cases of Professors that had to change Departments or quit Universities because of peer harassment, sometimes associated with bullying. Imagine Einstein rejected because he was a physicist instead of a mathematician, Relativity Theory would not be around. The evolution of science and society needs variety, those savant Professors should understand that.

The University is located in a Pleasure Valley, on the outskirts of the capital. It takes about half an hour to get there from downtown, without traffic. Jeremy used to drive a motorcycle those days and he was always punctual for his classes. The University is beautiful, lots of gardens and open spaces. It is a privilege to teach or study at that University. He wanted to meet some peers and started by visiting the cafeteria. It was the same round design with servers in the middle; one or two employees on the till collecting the money, and the others serving coffee or sandwich just beside. He ordered a coffee and sat at one of the cement chairs available. He was thinking about his experiences at the University, the people he met, the difficulties in teaching, and so on. Today, there are not even half the Professors that used to teach there, most of them left the country and started new careers someplace else with more potential to make their career.

He was sitting for a while but didn't see anybody he knew. He decided to walk toward Departmental Buildings, moving toward the

Artificial Intelligence Department, where he used to teach. There was a Professor he always appreciated and that had a good political understanding. He walked to the second floor and started to look up the names on the doors, he recognized some names, but he wanted to find out precisely the Andean Professor, the one born in the Andes and established at the capital many years ago. Finally, he found the door, knocked, but there was no answer, nobody was around.

He remembers this Andean Professor helping him to build up a database for a research many years ago. Jeremy made a form with many questions and multiple answers. He had difficulties analyzing 500 or 600 interviews and hundreds of questions per questionnaire. The Professor suggested using a simple database system, instead of a statistical package; it provided multiple analysis using equations like a spreadsheet. Jeremy visited him a few times while he was learning the tool and thanked him for the help. Jeremy was able to produce a paper that was sent to a known scientific magazine.

He stopped at the Secretary to ask for the professor, the lady said, "The Professor is in class, he should be back in half an hour." He decided to walk up and down the stairs see if somebody else was around, but the corridors were empty and the doors were closed. The explanation of the emptiness was simple. Many Professors had to work outside the University to complete a salary to feed their families. He recalled his experiences there, doing research, teaching, talking with Professors and Students, attending students' questions and going for coffee or lunch with peers.

He still remembers an anecdote with some Professors of the University. They went for lunch at the ranch on top of a hill, a married couple and another Professor. Jeremy was mentioning an experience at a Conference in Chicago. He remembered the Hotel in Downtown were the Conference was held. He arrived late in the afternoon and was hungry at the Hotel. Because it was still clear, he decided to stroll nearby and grab something to eat. He remembers going toward a street with some fast food restaurants; he was trying to decide where to eat. Sunset was starting, light was scarce, suddenly, he noticed everybody around him was not precisely white skinned, but the complete opposite, all were Afro-Americans. He started to feel uncomfortable by the way people moved. A few minutes before, he did not notice anything, there was a mix of races and suddenly everybody was black, acting strange, and the evening was getting darker.

Warn you that Jeremy has never been a racist at all he never said anything against blacks. He had some friends in Small Venice that were black. Why he felt uncomfortable with many black people in the street? He thought that those people hanging close to the wall and moving from one store to the next could be hazardous. He started to feel scared and decided to go back fast to the Hotel. He went to the Restaurant and grabbed something to eat. He felt alleviated and safe again.

The lady Professor was brown skinned and she felt alluded, she said that there was no reason to feel scared in that situation blacks in the US are not bad people, and so on. Her husband, that lived in the US a few years ago said more or less the same, blacks were good people, nothing to fear about. Jeremy understood his anecdote was not well received but maintained his viewpoint, he was not racist but he felt prudent to flee under the circumstances. It is an example of a common generalization. People think any situation must be understood always in the same way, that people are good in all cases, and worse of all, the racist argument, that blacks are rejected. For Jeremy it would not matter the color of the skin, even whites leaning on the walls and moving fast up and down the allies would be suspicious, Jeremy would had fled with whites too.

He finally spotted the Andean Professor, greeted him with affection and said, "Why don't we go for a coffee? I'm coming from a class and I need also some water, classes make me thirsty." They went down the stairs to the cafeteria and sat at the cement chairs. Jeremy explained what he was doing regarding games and society, and wanted more understanding about democracy. The Professor told Jeremy that the topic was not one he mastered fully and suggested to better contact another Professor of Political Sciences called Torregas located in an office at the Library. The Professor said the economic situation was serious and had to go downtown to attend another job where he started to make an additional income. This was the situation for most professors surviving at the expense of students. The Andean Professor told Jeremy to contact him through email, Twitter or Facebook, he will be more than happy to give some feedback on whatever Jeremy proposed.

He walked to the Library and asked for the Professor. The name Torregas was familiar but he didn't remember much about him. Jeremy found the office and the professor greeted him in, Jeremy recognized him immediately, he was a famous politician. Jeremy explained the reason for his visit. Torregas seemed happy to get somebody visiting him. Jeremy remembered when the professor participated in a Presidential election several years ago and he appeared on TV giving political opinions. He was third on the popular vote on those elections, he was the only civilian among the three candidates the other two came from the military. Now he worked mostly at the University.

Democracy is the most common form of government, explained Torregas, the society is institutionalized, powers are autonomous and the decisions are made with people's participation through representatives in the government. Mandates last certain periods of four or five years and those elected are not allowed to stay in power forever. Institutions are autonomous but supervised through levels of control. Democracy is so popular that even dictators call themselves democrats, presenting a legitimate picture smiling with their ministers.

Torregas has been associated to some independent parties and was an activist establishing new parties in the country. He seemed to be moving from one party to another over the years, he has been quite volatile. He moved back and forth like waves at sea, from the University to politics. This time he was trying to write some books about the situation in the country and his experiences with the deceased leader of the revolution.

Jeremy knew a dictatorship when he was a kid, remembers a parade where he marched in front of the dictator. He stayed hours waiting and the march itself lasted about one hour. He got so much sunburn that stayed red for a week. He also remembers the last days of the dictator, sending troops on the streets to scare people. At the time, Jeremy lived in a small house in the center of the capital and heard the troops marching close to his window, he didn't dare to open the window, he stayed quite while they passed by.

He knew there were problems in the country, but he was too young to understand what was happening and who was right or wrong. He remembers his father taking the picture of the dictator off the wall of the small cleaning shop they owned; owners were forced to keep the picture of the dictator in visible places of the stores. He knew later on that some employees of the Ministry of the dictatorship received cleaning services.

One of the biggest defects of a democracy, said Torregas, is the possibility of citizens to vote for an option without information or lack of knowledge about the implications of their decisions. In many occasions, people vote for a candidate without knowing her, the consequences of their choice, or understanding what the stakes are. Most people vote for a motion because somebody suggested them to do so or because it had been advertised, not because they have made some research about what was required. Few people are really conscious of their vote, most of the time it is superficial decision making.

SOCIALIST BINGO - Germinal Boloix

In many occasions, said Jeremy, people vote for sympathy or familiarity with some approach or candidate, but not because they are certain of what they do. Friendship and interest are always considered, sometimes people vote against an enemy or a distasteful choice. If democracy continues that way, societies are not going to solve their basic problems. As any other complex structure, democracy must be subject to scrutiny, it is not a Holy Grail.

In democracy, explained Torregas, popularity is a big decision making mechanism, people vote for a beautiful face, or a famous name, independently of the real merit of the candidate. Most people are superficial and politicians benefit from that reality. Take the case of a businessman or a military, persons without much preparation for a political job, but with lots of popularity. If we use their profession as the reference, they should never be considered candidates; however, if we talk about persons that took the time to learn political sciences, it would be possible to accept them. Candidates are usually well known persons in the community and independently of his political merits have been acclaimed for the job. Lots of people are going to vote for them in the next elections, some voters think they know what they do others follow the multitude or the tendencies. It is not a good idea to elect a businessman or military, they are not fit for the job, it is better to choose a philosopher instead they have a better perspective and lots of doubts.

If you want to be a contender, you need to appear in the news, social media, community forums, and so on. It is not a matter of being right or wrong but pure and simple popularity. In some cases popularity is increased because other candidates made the wrong pledges and lost popularity. Democracy has many advantages, but it also has many disadvantages. What happens in a close vote, 51% versus 49%? Why the 'majority' (50% plus one) wins and crushes the 'minority' (50% minus one)? Half and half means you have a problem, half the population is going to be happy while the other half is going to be unhappy. Half and half should mean you have to go back and convince at least half of the half to get three quarters of the vote. Two thirds or three fourths in favor might be an acceptable solution, but half and half is not.

Trying to give an example of vote counting, Jeremy took the case of an election: there are three candidates, all known by the voters in some way or another. How do you think the distribution of votes among candidates is going to be? Most of the time, it would be one third each. The reason is that the candidates are known by the voters. Other possible distributions generate results where those more popular are going to get more votes of course. It is a matter of popularity, "I know that candidate, appeared on TV." It is not that you know that one candidate is superior intellectually to the other and capable of performing well, No!, it is just that you have heard about him and it makes him affordable for your vote.

Let us take a conflictive example, establishing laws about abortion in terms of allowing it or not. A significant amount of people is going to agree and others are going to disagree. It is not convenient to make laws favoring one group against the other; the society must allow lapses of discussion to study the ethical consequences of abortion. The best thing is not to be sharp and general, but flexible and specific; it has to be established in which cases abortion could be allowed and in which denied; it has to be established what kind of psychological and economic support is going to be given to mothers, forced to take care of children that come into the world with some kind of rejection.

Absurd Socialism, according to Torregas, runs under a disguised democracy, it benefited from people's lack of interest on public matters and took power undeservedly. Absurd Socialism used the democratic institutions to get power and then, with time, started to change their democratic mask, becoming a real Orthodox Socialism government punishing the people.

If democracy is going to stay, said Jeremy, it is important to establish a knowledge base during the elections containing details of a candidate or option, presenting an informed opinion to the public. Research can be done by individuals or groups and should be published to bring it to the people; debates and discussion are necessary to build up political knowledge. Philosophers must take the lead and produce unbiased explanations that reach the general population. Philosophers and Intellectuals are the ones that must conquer the world, charlatans are unwelcome.

Torregas thought like a philosopher too, always doubting about reasonableness and moving from one party to the next according to his beliefs. He said that democracy is usually attached to capitalism to solve the economic problems. He said, "Money is an abstract concept, independently of his physical representation through coins and bills; besides, today everything is plastic as you know."

He continued saying that money is here to stay, that there is no way of getting rid of it. Not even the most socialist fanatics can live without it. The problem is how to manage the money, how to administer income and expenses, that is the question. The basic difference between political strategies is money management. Capitalism is totally different from socialism. One approach impulses free enterprises, the other seeks government subsidies for the population.

Torregas stated that the Absurd Socialism regime was improvising too much, it was not a copy of the Island, North Korea or China, or any other related regime, but it was a trial and error type of government that pushed their people down the cliff. Many citizens were experiencing their worst hunger dilemma in centuries.

Before saying good-bye, Torregas suggested Jeremy read several books he had published about the regime and about democracies in the world. Jeremy wrote the names of the books and thanked the professor. The conversation was fruitful, democracy is very important nowadays but it is full of defects that must be corrected. It is very important to forget about popularity contests in the selection of future leaders; democracy deserves the best-prepared people in positions of power.

Chapter 6: Society at Liberator Square

Jeremy was walking by Liberator Square, located in Downtown. The Square is quite famous, people used to visit it on weekends walking with their families, and having popcorn, ice cream, and candy. There is a huge equestrian sculpture of The Liberator on top of his horse located at the center of the Square. It is made in dark bronze with a marble pedestal, quite impressive, about five meters tall. The Liberator is the most important figure in the history of Small Venice. He came from a rich family and was capable of risking his life and fortune to liberate the country. Today people should risk their life to liberate Small Venice from the Socialist Dictatorship.

In recent years, some corners of the Square have been transformed in a refuge of political propaganda. People in favor of the government used to bother passersby with their propaganda in favor of the leader of the revolution. Jeremy used to pass by the Square for many years because he was teaching some courses nearby. The metro station is just one block away; it is the best transport in downtown. The Institution was about four blocks away from the square. Today, he was just going for a stroll, to find out how was it transformed, from a nice place to go and get amused into a propaganda center for the regime. He saw many people sitting here and there, but this time he didn't see any political groups bothering people.

A human society is a group of people, continued thinking Jeremy, involved in persistent interpersonal relations. A large social group sharing the same geographical or social territory, typically subject to the same political authority and dominant cultural expectations. People are characterized by patterns of relationships (social relations) between individuals who share a Culture and Institutions; a given society may be described as the total sum of such relationships among its constituent members. In the social sciences, a society often evinces stratification or dominance patterns in subgroups.

The society is a group of people that through mutual cooperation accomplishes the objectives of life. The society has laws that must be complied by citizens; laws should be written to increase the prosperity of citizens. The society is plagued with inequalities, some are born under better conditions than others. If you are a son of poor people, your opportunities of improvement will be reduced. Those born poor are going to have less chances of living better during their life span. Those born in wealthy families usually have better chances to live a prosperous life.

SOCIALIST BINGO - Germinal Boloix

Jeremy was born in a home of workers, there were no rich around. He had his opportunities in life, and he profited, mainly study and work. He thinks he had a good life, raising her daughters, sharing with his grandchildren, traveling en enjoying a bit, and retiring to accomplish his own philosophical interests. He would have liked to travel a bit more around the world but his financial limitations did not let him. He was always interested in being useful and contribute to society with his abilities. He never had a pure economical interest in the things he did; economic considerations were just collateral, even though decisive when there was a big imbalance that impacted his survival capability.

While walking near the Square, he spotted his fellow Professor Naveda, he still teaches some courses in the Institute, "How are you Naveda, long time without talking to you, what courses are you teaching now?"

"Hello. How are you? I'm good, busy doing many things. I am teaching at the Graduate level, mostly giving advice to students. I only teach one of my old courses on Computers and Society. You know how much technology changes in a couple of years and the effects on Society. It is difficult to stay up to date on all that new knowledge."

"Wow, you are the one I am looking for to try to understand some concepts about Society." Jeremy spent some time going through the main concepts, explained his approach to understanding a society and what he thought about politics and games.

Naveda is a nice guy, knows how to behave in the Institute political arena. He worked well with representatives of the opposition as well as those of the government, had some kind of empathy towards people, beyond politics. Jeremy had many anecdotes regarding old professors of the Institute; one is about 'Notee,' the nickname meaning 'No teeth' because he didn't seem to visit the dentist too often. When he smiled, a dark shadow on his left side demonstrated his lack of teeth. Another professor was called 'ears ponytail' because he had such a long hair on his ears that he could wear a ponytail. There was another that got gigantic packages of deodorant for his bad odor. Still other was dark skinned and smelt liquor when stepping down the stairs of the Institute.

"Why don't we go for a coffee and talk about all these concepts in the meantime. If you want a Strawberry Shortcake, I am willing to buy you some" said Jeremy.

"I thank you for the cake but I got diabetes type two and I cannot eat too much sugar. Let us go for the coffee instead; I know a place where espressos used to be excellent."

"Sure let us go," said Jeremy. "You know that the place where I found the better espresso was Italy. I was there a couple of years ago and anywhere you went the coffee was excellent."

"You are lucky having the opportunity to travel and drink the best coffees in the world. Here, in Small Venice, the coffee is not so good anymore, you know, the government is in charge of producing coffee, they use to mix it with wood and other stuff. Well, that is what we got, hope it is not bad on our tummy" said Naveda.

"That is true, we have to pay attention to what food we eat and what medicines we take people are getting intoxicated with food and medicines these days."

He recalls working with Naveda, they had a good time preparing the Curriculum, defining projects for the students or planning schedules for thesis exams. Jeremy found out that he had a good time working with him, that the job looked easy and amusing. In that Institution, Naveda was his best work companion. It is possible to say that they were like John Lennon and Paul McCartney from the Beatles, everything they composed was successful and they felt so happy with their work.

Many Professors tried research initiatives in the areas of multimedia, neural networks, software engineering; they had no chance to succeed because of the socialistic nature of the authorities. The Institute didn't appreciate the fundamental research, were suggesting applied research, oriented to solve problems for the community. This is the typical approach of socialistic regimes, instead of being open minded and allowing a variety of possibilities, they want everything oriented to social applications, limiting the freedom of research. In life you need some balance; variety is a gift well deserved.

Naveda reflected, "As you know, in Small Venice, a small group of lefties has taken power and benefited from the ignorance of the population on matters of what is a society well run. Besides, the military is in charge and the population is frightened."

"The society has an impact on individuals because it regulates their behavior; individuals are restrained by laws and cultural traditions, the government imposes restrictions."

"We all know how many companies have bankrupted in recent years because of a wrong economic strategy," said Naveda, repeating what everybody knows.

SOCIALIST BINGO - Germinal Boloix

More broadly, explained Naveda getting into the subject, a society may be illustrated as an economic, social, and industrial infrastructure, made up of a varied collection of individuals. On the other side, the society must be influenced by good politicians proposing better ways to run a society.

The definition of society brought into Jeremy's mind the usual problems happening in building condominiums. He thought it was a good analogy: society and condominiums. It reminded him the severe problems in the building he lived many years ago. In a condominium, there are several institutions: the janitor, security, maintenance, administration, legal matters, relations among neighbors and so on. The problems in condominiums are similar to those happening in a society, the owners want the condominium directors to exert all the functions while they just go in and out of the building. Neighbors are inconsiderate, they only know how to criticize but not how to collaborate. Let us add personal problems among neighbors and the situation becomes a time bomb. The similarity between the society and the condominium is remarkable, in a society happens the same, people go to work, provide for their family and sit comfortably observing from home what happens in the country; it is not their problem whether the government is bad, they wait for the elections to change them, but they do not demand immediate improvements, they are totally passive.

Naveda found the analogy totally appropriate, he thought it was better than the analogy between family and society, that is also possible. That is why he said that while groups of neighbors do not apply direct action, nothing is going to happen in the condominium or society. It is a utopia to believe that all the neighbors are going to get involved, it is enough with a numerous group to exert pressure and achieve the needed changes. Why a condominium directive stays for years without presenting results on revenues and expenses and without performing the needed maintenance in the building. The same thing happens in societies, governments do not give accounts, do not produce, and do not solve anything.

Naveda wanted to introduce an important topic, a cultural component that makes the difference, each country can have a particular vision totally different in similar subjects. It is well known that there are countries where people do not accept irregularities, there are pressure groups in the society that demand their rights and they do it in full voice. If the institutions are not complying, these groups do intervene and make the society to follow an appropriate course.

Thinking about the country's culture, Jeremy said, "You know how difficult it is to get rid of such a bad regime governing our country these days. People want politicians to make decisions and politicians want people involved in political tasks."

"When the government dominates politically all the Institutions, it can do whatever it wants, even destroy the country in front of your eyes. It is a disgrace to manage the country as a grocery store, the owner deciding what to sell and at what price, instead of promoting the free market." Naveda understood that without people's participation changes are impossible.

There is one aspect that has worried me for long time, said Jeremy, society is like a monster with a thousand heads and each one pulls its way. Governments use to have a predefined agenda that does not follow the population desires, they go their way and people follow a different route. Additionally, citizens have no communication channels to vent their preoccupations. Citizens have their own vision about how the society must work and in practice they find many obstacles. When somebody disagrees with a norm, there is no way to present arguments to abolish or change it. On the other side, governments do not seem interested in listening to citizens, they want to follow their work program blindly, like unintelligent machines.

Naveda was listening casually, he seemed to recognize a common preoccupation in the society. After a few instants, he explained to Jeremy that he was right, that many citizens do not find ways to intervene in the current norms, that they are frustrated for the separation between them an the decision makers. All societies suffer from these weaknesses, but there are some that try to keep constant contact with their citizens to intervene on time to improve society.

Modern societies should not be oppressive to the individual, on the contrary, a society should improve and adapt to the requirements of individuals. Jeremy showed his individualist concerns, where collectivities are created around individuals. There is not just one collectivity, there can be many. For Jeremy, the collectivity versus individuality issue is paramount. The term collectivity is an abstraction to put everybody under the same umbrella. If the collectivity performs well, everybody is happy but if it does not, nobody can be pointed out. Let us take the case of a Police Department, if they perform well, citizens are happy but if they kill innocent people, citizens complain. The fault is going to be attached to the Police as a generic term whereas the problem was a policeman mistake or wrongdoing. In a society, the term collectivity generalizes everybody under the same pattern of needs, knowledge, income, and so on. Everybody knows there are differences among individuals, therefore, it is unjust to put everybody under the same viewpoint.

"The problem in Small Venice is that the leaders want to stay in power just to benefit from the country's oil income or to be important staying in the limelight," said Naveda, thinking on how egoism affects individuals.

"Other aspect is that individuals are not equal, and the regime has the tendency to put everybody under the same roof; unprepared laborers in charge of managing big enterprises without appropriate knowledge," said Jeremy remembering anarchism.

He felt on his terrain, his parents were workers fighting for their rights and added, "Participation is not wrong, what is wrong is forced participation, as to complete a quota, saying that laborers are the owners by law, independently of how capable they are."

"It is the old Marxist dream of Proletariat Dictatorship, where the laborers become the masters and the masters become the slaves." Said Naveda, that was a Marxist many years ago, and he agrees laborers must be doing their chores, distinct than strategical and managerial responsibilities in the enterprise.

In sociology, continued Naveda, social capital is the expected collective or economic benefits derived from the preferential treatment and cooperation between individuals and groups. Social networks provide value and services to society. Social capital can be measured by the amount of trust and 'reciprocity' in a community or between individuals. Today, the regime has concentrated all the services in the State, saying that they are going to be in charge of all the production activities. "According to my experience, this regime has not improved the social capital, we are worse than Haiti."

After 18 years in power, Jeremy explained, the socialists have demonstrated to be a disaster. The networks of production and distribution have been dismantled by decree, hunger and scarcity are going to grow and people are going to die. It is on purpose that the regime eliminates private production and distribution networks; they want total loyalty from the people, up to the point of kneeling, begging for food and medicines. It is embarrassing.

Human capital, added Naveda, from the point of view of the individual, is the stock of competencies, knowledge, habits, social and personality attributes, including creativity, cognitive abilities, embodied in the ability to perform labor so as to produce economic value. Human capital takes into consideration the importance of the individual instead of the collective. Taken together, Social and Human Capital, they define the potential of the production and distribution networks in a community. "If human capital is high, but the social capital is low, there is no advantage for society."

Naveda stated, "Collectivism views the group as the primary entity, with the individuals lost along the way, clustering them to become a massive group. It is possible to say that socialists do this to simplify things, they do not want to bother too much on differences, and apply equality indiscriminately."

Collectivists have closely linked individuals, continued Naveda, who view themselves primarily as parts of a whole, be it a family, a network of co-workers, a tribe, or a nation. The group has its own values, somehow different from those of the individual members. The group determines its own thoughts and beliefs. Instead of judging the group as a bunch of individuals interacting, it judges the group as a whole and views the individuals thinking similarly. It's true that people grow up within a culture, but they are free to accept or reject its mandate. Being a part of these groups doesn't make you act the way they force you. That's up to the people free will should still be an option.

"Yes, but individuals that don't comply with the regime are going to suffer discrimination. If you have a family to raise, better get on the train of the regime, unless you want them to starve" said Jeremy. He has always been a rebel promoting the free opinion, socialists do not appreciate rebellion.

Naveda agreed, "Of course, many people have suffered during these years, the regime is basically a disguised dictatorship, controlling all the production and all the Institutions."

"What form of a society shall we strive for?" asked Jeremy, starting to get anxious about solutions.

"Perhaps for none, there is no much difference among them. Culture determines society, not the other way around. Many philosophers, including Plato, have already suggested a government by men of merit and honor, every man, and woman according to their ability, but not to incompetence." Naveda answered.

"In this statement, there is an implicit elite view in charge. And the elite may be all wrong too. I would say that what is needed is prepared people, those that can manage and have the will to make things better, capable of organizing the country to produce prosperity for all." Jeremy was thinking either about the need of intellectuals doing the theoretical job.

"Of course, if people are not educated, trial and error become the tools of trade, and we all know that trial and error is costly and may take generations." Naveda continued.

"Think before acting is the better strategy." Thought Jeremy, like a good philosopher.

Those that have no imagination, said Naveda, are incapable of governing a country, are incapable of foreseeing the future. According to Plato, in The Republic, any human individual is at their best when they are pursuing what they are most capable of. For instance, an athlete should pursue physical excellence, an artisan should pursue excellence in their craft, and a leader should pursue justice.

Individuals must maintain a balance in three areas:
- Reason, (mind and intellect) which seeks the truth;
- Spirit, (will and volition) which seeks honor;
- Appetite, (desire and emotion) which seeks material goods (safety, food, drink, sex, and money)

In Plato's model, there are three main classes of actors in the State:
- The Guardians, who love knowledge and truth above all. They rule the State.
- The Auxiliaries, who love courage, honor, and their homeland above all. They defend the State.
- The Producers, who love fruits of their labors, security, comfort, and material well-being above all. They provide the material and functional needs of the State.

Present throughout Plato's work is the juxtaposition of appearance and reality. Plato is eager to show that we cannot judge truth on the basis of what it appears to be. We need reason and questioning to get beyond appearance and closer to the truth.

Jeremy, that had read The Republic too, said, "Plato's book, deals with practical issues such as the nature of justice, the human condition, and the basis of societal order and political power. Why modern societies do not follow those recommendations?"

He explained that according to Tomas Hobbes, cooperation could not develop without a central authority, and a strong government is necessary:

the commonwealth. Hobbes wrote Leviathan, introducing the life of men without government, living in a perpetual state of war, in constant fear and anxiety. Thus, a State or Commonwealth is required with the sole purpose of protecting the life of those who live in it. The citizens have obligations to this State. The obedience to the State is not in conflict with divine laws, for proper of God is to obey civil laws. Those that do not accept to live in the new State are condemned to live in Darkness. The need for a government seems guaranteed. However, what is not acceptable is to have everything, production, distribution, and the Constitution, concentrated in the hands of the government. Production and distribution can be handled by private enterprises, letting the government controlling or regulatory functions only; the Constitution must be managed by independent powers that seek justice.

Naveda added, "Controlling and regulatory functions seem more than enough responsibilities for a government. Why do they want to concentrate so much power with their bureaucracy?"

"The socialist regime wants to perpetuate in power, passing their power to new generations, from fathers to sons or daughters, and then to grandsons and granddaughters. It looks like an Aristocratic form of socialism."

With his natural educational instinct, Naveda wanted to help Jeremy in his research and suggested, "According to what you have presented, you need a framework or model to structure the notion of a society. To me, the key words for a society are justice and production."

Justice involves fairness, law, and order, continued Naveda. Production includes all the activities required by a society to benefit its citizens, such as supplying food, medicines, supplies, appliances, and several other types of services. There are actors that belong to the community, the people; there are facilities that include buildings, factories, hospitals, schools, and highways. Some example activities are education, health, transportation, recreation, communication, and technology.

"What makes a socialist society different from a capitalist one?" asked Jeremy. Do they have different objectives? Or the objectives are the same but the means are different? The objectives of any society, thought Jeremy, should be equivalent, but there is the individual versus the collective viewpoint and the pure financial gain versus the socialist welfare that makes a difference.

Naveda added, "I believe any society should provide prosperity to their citizens, independently of the political approach. A society that doesn't prosper is condemned to destruction. The notion of prosperity must be the heart and soul of any society."

"That is one serious setback of socialism it has not yet demonstrated its feasibility. Everything they suggest is trial and error" said Jeremy, that could not stand an improvising socialist regime.

Before leaving Naveda, Jeremy though about some complaints professors had in the Institute and they talk a bit about those issues. When the new orthodox socialist regime took charge of the Institute, a few years after the leader of the revolution took charge, the first thing they did was to benefit their supporters and penalize the opposition. Because many professors had always criticized the government, they were well known in the Institute. Jeremy recalls an event, during the oil strike, when some professors offered to hijack the directors of the Professors' Union because they said that nothing was happening at the Institute when, in reality, everybody was on strike. The faces of the socialist directors looked surprised by the professors' menaces, they looked ridicule.

In another case, the Authorities opened a concourse to distribute permanent jobs and give tenure positions. Many opposing professors that were in a full-time contractual basis were offered only jobs at a half or part-time positions because they were not loyal to the socialistic party. At the time, a famous Professor, looking alike Carlos Santana the famous guitarist, was related to the concourse, and in charge of the Department. He was not capable of suggesting a way for those professors to get the full-time job they deserved after working for many years on a contractual full-time basis. The professors complained to the authorities but they lied, saying that the mistake could be solved later, once the positions were given. At the end, the professors got only part-time positions that weren't enough to pay their bills.

According to Jeremy, the Professor could have given them the advice of protesting to the Education Ministry and obtain an injunction to stop the concourse and review the part-time versus full-time issue. Jeremy couldn't forget this mismanaged opportunity, these professor's unwelcome destiny is going to last forever.

The other Professor in charge of the Institution is a lady that is radical in favor of the leader of the revolution. She looks physically like the wife of the black president of the Giant of the North; but quite mean, she had no empathy toward human beings. She had no shame chasing opposing Professors, harassing them without pity. Once, she argued with some Professors telling them that their ID number was incorrect on certain documents, she had checked on the database. She used the information to find out which Professors had signed against the leader of the revolution and punishing them according to the Discriminating List objectives. It is incredible that an Educational Institution, that should promote multiple viewpoints, be capable of performing cheating and short minded actions; those discriminative Professors should not be part of the community.

The regime utilized political discrimination to crush the opposition. Jeremy's friends were seriously wounded by bureaucrats of the regime, "I remember how badly people got hurt by the actions of administrators of Public Institutions, they basically dismissed workers for their political viewpoint" Jeremy remembered.

His friends agreed, "It was awful, incredible according to human rights standards. Discriminating because of people's ideas is intolerable."

In the years of democracy, before the socialist's regime, it was not so harmful to be against the political party in power, those were the years where discrimination was not so severe. The leader of the revolution started a serious persecution against the opponents of the regime; his accomplices were in all public Institutions. Ideals discrimination is the worst type of discrimination a human being can suffer; it is preferable to be discriminated because of being black, or poor, or having no money to buy commodities than to be discriminated because you oppose a bad regime. The leader of the revolution discriminated opponents not letting them get jobs or services such as gas supply and lately reducing access to regulated food, by creating long lines and providing food packages only if you registered in the government patriots lists.

Jeremy's daily experiences represent the common way of living of many citizens of the country. Reasoning about the way people think about life and what is just or unjust provides a framework for understanding the day to day difficulties. As humans, we search more or less the same objectives: living, prospering, educating, recognizing, and contributing to society. It shouldn't matter what political regime we live in, we all want to live better. It is not acceptable to bring the whole population toward a cliff if socialists do not accomplish we must get rid of them.

Capitalism has many disadvantages, but socialism is worse. socialism is not viable, has no strong conceptual framework. They do not take into consideration human nature, with all its defects, differences, and variety; they want everybody to be equal to certain imaginary standard, invented by bureaucrats in power. Consider money, there is no country in the world that can function without it, money is the excrement of the devil. However, Socialists still keep the notion of money and profits, the capital is there and they accept it. "I want the price of the oil barrel to be more than 50 dollars," said the President. Socialism and capitalism require money to survive why do Socialist believe that they can live without the perverse influence of money?

Some of Jeremy's friends don't agree with capitalism oriented to increase the amount of money you have in the bank. They wish a type of capitalism creating jobs, giving opportunities to work and make people prosperous. Nobody is pushing capitalism as the solution, but it is better than socialism.

Reflecting on the conversation with Naveda, a well-administered society requires acknowledging those that provide forces for improvement. The government must be composed of men and women capable of performing their duties.

Chapter 7: Politics at Central University

Nuyma is a friend of Jeremy since she was a child. Her parents used to get together most weekends going to their home or going to the beach. He remembers primarily experiences going for a day to nearest beaches; swimming in the beach, hanging out on trees and going for short walks in the nearby mountains. Nuyma's father used to sell imported foods that he distributed for local supermarkets; it was a business that gave him the possibility to live well, nothing else; the gentleman used to visit his father at the cleaner's shop and they talked about different things, politics or otherwise.

One anecdote about Nuyma is that she was in love with Jeremy since she was young, but Jeremy wasn't interested in her at all. Jeremy remembers some of her girlfriends that he used to like more than Nuyma herself. Nuyma was strong and used to eat a lot, she swallowed a full tomato in just one bite, imagine, apples or pears, they didn't last long in the kitchen. Never mind, today Jeremy was interested in talking about socialism and capitalism.

She studied Sociology at the University, was a good candidate to give some feedback on political strategies to explain Small Venice sufferings. She is teaching at the University and doing some research in her domain. Jeremy contacted her and they met at the Central University, in one of the corridors where people use to walk and hang out. Jeremy also studied at the same University; it was great to have the chance to visit his old University again. The University has been named Humanity Patrimony because of its beautiful design. It has open spaces and gardens that make it unique, the buildings were built from a creativity perspective. After saying hello and talking about their parents, Jeremy started to present his point of view.

Regarding politics and society, asked Jeremy, why a bad regime, such as the one in Small Venice, can be in power and people do not complain strongly. Socialism is not a regime that promotes wellbeing, it promotes misery instead; this year the country occupies the last spot in a misery index based on growth and inflation. It is untrue that socialism is for the good of the poor instead, it is for the good of a minority in power. The only thing they look for is to be important and stay in power; some officers also want to touch some money and become rich, contradicting the social approach.

"Society is like a very complex organism, there is no political strategy capable of solving the problems of human beings." Started Nuyma, convinced of what she said.

"But there is some negative connotation on your comments, implying there is no solution." Said Jeremy a bit worried.

"I still have some hope, but poverty is there to stay and for long." Said Nuyma sadly, demonstrating that she was aware of so many penuries.

Jeremy presented some of his ideas about a society and explained that orthodox socialist regimes are not an alternative in a modern world. There are too many implications in having a government in charge of all the Institutions in a country without a minimum of regulation, negative feedback, and control. Additionally, the regime has demonstrated that total control was counterproductive.

Socialism is a beautiful word, but social benefits are not among its objectives; it makes people believe in helping those that have less, those that suffer, but in reality, it hides injustice. Everybody must go through the same path that has not demonstrated possibilities of success.

Money is always going to be present in the society, it is unavoidable. Thus, it does not matter the political system, money allows simplifying the exchange of services. It does not matter which activity to perform, money allows acquiring equipments, supplies and the hire employees needed for execution. The problem of socialists is that they believe that productive activities do not need money, that people work voluntarily without getting an income to buy food and pay bills.

"Jeremy, I believe many people have studied the feasibility of socialism, but the problems are in the interpretation of that knowledge. Governments start implementing strategies without a real understanding of what they do or what are the implications of their measures; people pay for that lack of knowledge" said Nuyma still defending a wrong approach.

"According to that socialism should not be an alternative at all because it depends on the government, it has no solid criteria." Jeremy remembers the government projects that get updated again and again without improving the country. One example is the system of currency exchange control, there have been more than twenty systems and nothing works.

Other negative comments about socialism, continued Jeremy, are that it promotes flattening everybody at the same low-income level, independently of their effort, contribution or merits. Socialism believes in rough equality, everybody deserves the same independently of their contribution; merits are not part of the equation. In socialism, collectivities and solidarity are misused concepts and the notions of individuality and freedom are not in their vocabulary. Additionally, socialism is authoritarian, the state forces you to do what they decide in their politburo.

"The evolution of socialism moves toward more freedom of enterprises, watch what is going on in China, where the economy is run under a capitalistic strategy," said Nuyma looking defensive to socialism.

"But in China people do not live well as far as I know. According to your comments, everything is an experiment, they may or not succeed" said Jeremy.

"If governments don't know what they do, imagine what happen in the mind of people with so much improvisation. Mental hospitals would become full of perturbed citizens." Said Nuyma worried about so many people depressed or suffering anxiety in Small Venice.

According to Jeremy, sometimes, people's lack of knowledge about socialism is not their fault, they are too busy surviving, or doing other things unrelated to politics. Most of the time, it's the fault of the circumstances, the context, or the government. 'Smart' politicians benefit from that sort of passive ignorance, working hard on popularity contests to attract voters.

Nuyma said, "It is relative, people must be autonomous, therefore they have to make up their mind. It's not a good idea to blindly blame politicians, people are also responsible for those disasters going on in a country."

"You know that most people do not want to worry about politics, they want an easy life and that everything around them runs smoothly," said Jeremy that knows how easy going people are.

Contrasting socialism with capitalism, said Jeremy, the latter is presented by detractors as the inferno of egoism, where everything depends on economic interest, where solidarity is not allowed, where the rich enjoy watching the poor die. Capitalism, with all its defects, is the best-known system of economic interchanges. However, it is worth to clarify that capitalism is motorized by money, if you have it you can undertake many productive businesses and benefit from the economic and political power. Of course, it is not fair to be important or powerful because of having money; many have no culture but have money and benefit from others. Capitalism is also authoritarian, you hire people to do what you order them to do, you feel in command without consideration to others. But do not forget that socialists threaten employees with layoff if they do not participate in acts to defend the government. Usually, philosophers are poor and have less room for maneuver to accomplish some objective in society, but they are neutral and punish nobody.

"The problem with capitalism is that it has not resolved the problems of the society. Therefore, people believe that there can be some other alternative and they want to give it a try." Said Nuyma suggesting that is better to try something new instead of keeping what you have.

It is not a good idea to do trial and error, said Jeremy. Change to get worst is not a good solution. It is not casual that capitalism keeps functioning in most countries, while socialism has had no real examples in the modern world; any real example of socialism implies a dictatorship. A possible explanation of capitalism success would be: it is a practical way of economic transactions that allows people to live, produce and get benefits following the rules of the society and take into consideration efforts and merits; idleness is penalized with poverty by the capitalistic system.

She was a kind of Socialist fanatic and sadly said, "It is a pity that socialism has not produced a running, successful society. That is why capitalism stays around powerful under the actual world circumstances."

Capitalism must be productive to be useful, believes Jeremy, generating jobs and promoting prosperity for the whole population. Pure financial benefits address increased capital and prosperity for the powerful.

"In the same way that you are a fanatic against socialism, there are people that are fanatics in favor of socialism." Nuyma continued. She did not understand that Jeremy was not really a fanatic; he was a scientist trying to demonstrate objectively the disadvantages of socialism.

"That reminds me of a reading I did a few years ago, that liberals and conservatives are naturally born. Therefore, many people are going to favor socialism, in the same way, many others aspire to capitalism," said Jeremy.

Jeremy did not agree with socialist born individuals. He thought socialists were very superficial and did not understand the need of making some individual effort. Socialists act like a matriarchal society, they protect too much others. I prefer autonomy of criteria and effort.

A silence was felt in the environment, Jeremy watched Nuyma, and she watched him back. One alternative was to change the subject a little bit. Jeremy suggested the possibility of talking about alternatives to socialism.

Social democracy, said Nuyma, is an alternative to revolutionary or orthodox Marxism. It aims at curbing inequality and poverty, providing public services such as care for the elderly, child care, education, health care, and workers compensation.

Jeremy disagreed saying, "I have no doubt that most of the policies associated with social democracy are healthy. However, I still disapprove the final objective of creating a socialist society; human beings do not deserve such a punishment. I believe strongly in the individual, all these socialist movements tend to thwart freedom."

Nuyma said, "It is a difficult topic, I expect some university students to start doing some research on that socialist contradiction. The rights secured by justice are not subject to political bargaining or to the calculus of social interest. Truth and justice are uncompromising to social and political interests."

Jeremy was never a socialist or a communist, there were some examples of countries following that route and he was adamant to accept that wrongful approach. He studied the characteristics of socialism and communism but he didn't spend lots of time when he was young, he was too busy studying and working. Today as a mature man, he is capable of taking some time browsing different political books and establishing the weakness of socialism.

It would be possible to propose an a very simplified example of investing in a business for 100 millions Pesos for several years, without considering many factors such as inflation, taxes, depreciation, or payment of interests. Let us say that the business produces 30% earnings, about 30 millions Pesos per year. It requires to hire ten workers earning one million Pesos per year, times ten workers means 10 millions Pesos per year. Just one capitalist investing 100 millions, would earn enough, let us say 10 millions per year, to live comfortably, possibly to save, and recover his investment in ten years, 10 millions per year. Let us remember that if the activity fails, the capitalist is going to lose his money, that is why he is going to make a commitment and avoid losses.

Now, let us say that a group of 10 socialists people get together for the same business producing 30 %, each must invest 10 millions to make the 100 millions capital budget. Everybody knows that workers lack capital, where are they going to find the money? Let us say that the socialist government gives them a loan without interest, they have to pay back the money, of course. If each socialist persons earns two millions in salary per year, double than in the case of the capitalist, it means 20 millions per year, and they could pay the debt also in ten years, paying ten millions per year. This socialist scheme looks quite attractive, workers are going to earn double compared with the capitalist scheme. Why this does not happen in reality? First, governments have not enough money to offer to citizens. The national budget in the country is 8 billions Pesos in 2017; one 8 followed with 12 zeros. That amount would allow to found 80 thousand similar business for 800 thousand persons only; the country has around 35 million inhabitants. However, like that, the government would be incapable of investing money in anything else; therefore it is impossible to spend all the budget to serve workers. Second, founding activities requires creativity and knowledge, therefore, founding 80 thousand new activities is almost impossible; workers are not characterized for inventing new productive activities. Additionally, remember that if the activity fails, the government loses the money, we, the citizens, are all going to lose the money because it belong to all of us.

With this simplified example, has been demonstrated that there is no way for governments to finance socialists partners to generate productive activities to improve the life of persons. Capitalists are usually more creative at the time of founding new productive activities. Therefore, the saving during years of people is required, they may take a chance of investing in business that would allow a better life and the capability to prosper. A capitalist takes care of his company while a socialist does not care about common instalations.

Nuyma is not a lover of economic accounts, but she understood that without capital is not possible to start any activity in capitalism or socialism. Governments are not so rich such as to promote business for all; knowledge and creativity, normally, are not generated by the working class, thinking minds are required. Private initiative is always important and it has to be allowed, entrepreneurs should not be suffocated and they require more freedom to be able to invent. Additionally, capitalists risk their money in those activities; the government can dedicate its effort to social and community work.

Why a socialist government is still in power, even though a majority of the country is rejecting it right now. That was Jeremy's preoccupation. The regime has locked down all possibilities of replacement and is not obeying the Constitution. They are using the judicial system to avoid any rational society saving intervention. The government has minimal popularity and should relinquish power, they have done an extremely bad job. According to some news, the government has less than 20% approval rate. Jeremy does not believe it, it should be much less, but it is real according to the companies that make the surveys.

"The government of Small Venice is one of the worst of our history, and I remind you that the situation worsened these last three years. Probably the meltdown of oil prices had a big impact. When the leader of the revolution was there, the situation was not so bad." Nuyma said in a comprehensive note.

Without showing off his anger, Jeremy replied, "I do not believe it was because of him being in power, it was because he had too much money to do whatever he wanted."

She agreed, "Of course you are right, but try to say that to the people, they are not going to believe in you at all. They believe that the leader was very intelligent and capable of solving any problem. We all know that this was not true, he was a myth."

It was bad luck to be so close to the new socialist regime that governs Small Venice. Jeremy remembers the leader of the revolution when he just started in power and had enormous support. He saw him on TV during his 'Hello President' programs almost every weekend. After watching him during three weeks he said, "Why people are supporting this guy? It is evident that the guy has nothing in the ball (analogy to baseball), besides, coming from the military gives you an idea of how short minded he is regarding social issues. His higher responsibility was supervising a military cafeteria." Why people have elected this guy, somebody that is not qualified to run the country. Usually, people elect presidents that are more qualified than themselves. It seems many citizens considered him to be their image, came from the poor and so many other twisted criteria. Jeremy knows many Institutions around the world and there are brilliant and mediocre people around. However, in the military, brilliance is not a characteristic to be looked after; they use to prefer loyalty and obedience instead.

"I believe it is Small Venice people's idiosyncrasy that makes a difference. If people were different, they had never elected an incapable person." Nuyma said unexpectedly.

Plato already suggested that military and businessmen shouldn't govern a country, said Jeremy; they are not fit for the job. That reminded him the current case of 'Blondie' running for the presidency of the Giant of the North, another incapable that has delusions of grandeur. Jeremy thought, "Why people are going to vote for a guy that is not fit for a government office and with so many defects? I hope the 'Lady' becomes the President instead."

SOCIALIST BINGO - Germinal Boloix

Nuyma thought differently, "You see, 'Blondie' could be the next President of the Giant of the North, independently of what you say. There always are people with a twisted mind."

Talking about 'Blondie' brought up Jeremy's old memoirs, when he was younger and believed on the Island's Revolution. A few years before marrying, he had a poster of the Dictator of the Island in his room, somebody gave it to him, and his Mom said, "Listen, that guy has killed thousands of defectors of his regime, it is a criminal, how do you keep that poster in your room?" Jeremy did not move the poster in the following weeks but it disappeared afterward, he took it away, independently of believing on the Island's Revolution or not.

There is a serious problem in the world, people prefer charlatans instead of philosophers. Charlatans are immature and superficial, they talk and talk, and make the wrong decisions systematically. 'Blondie' in the Giant of the North, 'Bearded' in the Island and the 'leader of the revolution' in Small Venice, all big liars and charlatans. Why are people so blind? It would be acceptable a short empathy at the beginning, but after a few months or maximum a year, people must react and drop their support to charlatans.

A society shouldn't be run with socialistic principles, said Jeremy, they are anti-democratic; they chase individuals away from its natural behavior, don't allow freedom of action or speech. Limitations of freedom are conclusive to society failure; a straitjacket imposed on individuals is too restrictive for the productivity of a society. Socialist regimes empower the judicial system to embarrass individuals and avoid innovation.

Remembering her childhood, Nuyma said, "It is the same case of parents that punish physically their children. Most people don't agree, but there are some still applying detestable approaches. Humans are born free and should keep their autonomy without pressure from society."

It would be possible to say that in life, thought Jeremy, the capitalistic approach is superior, but many people still believe in fantasy and look up for utopias. It is not casual that the capitalistic approach has been around for so many years, there must be a natural reason.

"However, we all know that capitalism has not been able to demonstrate absolute mastery of the society, has not provided continuous growth; capitalism should be improved on its weaknesses to stay in power," Nuyma said feeling powerful.

"But the solution is not to replace blindfolded capitalism with socialism."

Nuyma said, "In life, any government should have more or less the same objective: to help the population. Independently of socialistic or capitalistic approaches, the main objective is to increase wellbeing and prosperity."

We know how different a socialistic regime is compared to a capitalistic one, said Jeremy. However, Absurd Socialism is the worst example of a socialistic regime, an oil producer country that now produces hunger on the streets. People look for food into the garbage cans continuously; before, you saw cans' pick up but today is hunger.

Steve Jobs

Steve Jobs was an intelligent and creative man, he had some motivational driving force that produced changes in our daily lives, the world needs people like him. Steve Jobs has been criticized on his dominant personality it is not the man that we have to criticize, but his ideas, the results, and his contribution that matters. Men and women are full of personal defects, but the strength and perseverance of their actions, accompanied by excellent results, make the difference. Steve Jobs stated his ideas for successful technological projects, taking into consideration all the aspects surrounding a project, proposing solutions that contribute to improving human activities.

Jeremy recalls a video presenting Steve Jobs, the mastermind behind Apple Computers. Steve presents his view of a successful product: the contents of the product must be the driving force behind any technological development. Put the best professional team together, give them support, and the best product can be developed. When objectives, different from the product are considered, it sidelines from objectives and the quality is deceiving. If we only seek economic benefits or marketing simplicity, the product is hurt and its usefulness diminishes.

The world needs innovation to be able to eliminate hunger and promote prosperity; it is not socialism the one to improve production processes, it is the free enterprise that would collaborate with the human race. Socialism is the same as living during the dark ages of humanity, between the fifth century and the first millennium, five hundred years of retardation for humanity. Innovation is only possible within 'productive capitalism.' The objective would be to regulate capitalism and create a better world.

Socialism, according to Jeremy, is an absolutely lost approach, it doesn't promote innovation and doesn't appreciate the effort put into new gadgets. Marx wrote his book taking laborers as the most important component of commodities, but he forgot the importance of commodities themselves. Jeremy has known many socialist that believe that things are free, that the effort of somebody else doesn't need any consideration. For example, socialist governments don't hire computers programmers because they believe that software must be free, that they don't have to pay for the effort put into the development of a system or computer application, it is already built, why pay for it!

At the end of the conversation, Jeremy asked Nuyma about her private life, "Did you ever marry?"

"You know that I didn't, I was in love with you and you were not interested in me, what could I do?"

"I am sorry Nuyma, but my sentimental life made me act that way, I didn't feel in love with you, you were like part of my family. Love is felt or is not, it cannot be faked."

Nuyma saw Jeremy with affection and recognized that life is not as easy as a fairy tale.

Reflecting on the conversation with Nuyma, politics are necessary for a society, however, bad politicians are making too much damage. The political strategy has an impact on our wellbeing do not let mediocrity get in power. Capitalism is not the best economic system but is superior to socialism with its ignorant collectivity paradigm.

Chapter 8: Devil's Advocate

While at Beach Town, Jeremy uses to contact his friend Gabriel that lives just half an hour away. He owns a little farm close to a town the same size as Beach Town. He has been working on the farm for at least ten years since he started to retire. Jeremy knew Gabriel at University level and studied the same Engineering career. The university experience is one of the bests in life, even though you do not pay attention while there. The stress of keeping up learning the material makes life a day after day struggle. Worrying about courses and future work expectations makes time pass by relatively fast. University is like a job where you have to respond promptly.

At the time, he remembers going for a ride to the beach with some friends towards the east side shore in an old car, and because he was not speeding, one friend said: "It is the first time in my life that I have had the time to enjoy this beautiful shore, waves striking giant rocks floating in the sea and the beautiful mix of blue and green colors." Time was always available, primarily during vacations and holidays, but sometimes you had to remain sleepless to catch up with university responsibilities.

During a physics exam with a hypothetical situation of a bird standing up inside an empty no air crystal cage, Jeremy recognized who Gabriel was. The cage was on top of a balance that measured the weight. The question was how the weight on the balance would change when the bird starts flying? Most students answered that the balance weight was reduced by the bird's weight when flying; some said the bird couldn't fly without air; others said the balance didn't change because of the bird's flying feathers pushed down the same weight. Gabriel answered that the bird should be dead by now, because there was no air, therefore it couldn't fly and there was no change in the balance. The Professor commented the answer and gave him full credits. Jeremy was impressed by this demonstration of inside no other student gave the same answer.

He was thinking about how disgusting it was to terminate a relationship with friends or family. Why in more than one occasion, when someone mentioned the possibility of breaking up, it really happened. For Jeremy, personal relationships, between friends, family members, work companions or other nearby citizens, means different values, for example, responsibility, solidarity, and loyalty. Each relationship has its degrees of values; the degree of responsibility with family is greater than with friends. Solidarity may change over time, favoring some and penalizing others. Loyalty can be expressed in some relationships or totally forgotten in others.

Human beings are weak, some fail in responsibility, others in solidarity, and others in loyalty. Human weaknesses determine our difficulties, some are disrespectful, some are unfriendly, some need company, some love nobody, some believe they are saviors, some get sold by money, some do not accept their lover to leave them, and so on. With so many defects, it is impossible that a society advance and progress.

Friendship can be thought as beautiful-butterflies' watching. They fly next to you showing their colors, may stop on a branch, and you go running to watch them. You enjoy their company, you may spend time astonished establishing their color structure; you may even want to catch and keep them forever. Each time you see them again you enjoy their company, time flies by; friendship is agreeable, butterflies too. Every now and then you want to see them again to enjoy that nice vision or company.

As any other type of personal relationship, friendship requires taking care of, trying to avoid conflictive situations; sometimes an excess of confidence may produce a lack of respect toward others. However, breaking up a friendship, if it is justified, usually doesn't hurt much, you may not care, or you can let it go altogether, even though you enjoyed friends so much; when break up comes up, you do not miss it much, eventually you forget about it and try to get a new one.

About friendship, Jeremy has a particular viewpoint. He has always thought that friends are made to enjoy life, and not to benefit from them. He remembers many times when he had economic difficulties and he never suggested to his friends borrowing or asking a service from them. Many years ago he had to make an improvement in his apartment and needed about 3 or 4 million old Pesos, and his monthly salary was around 2 million old Pesos. Jeremy had one close friend that was making around 7 or 8 million old Pesos at the time, his friend could spare 1 or 2 million to help him, but he didn't dare to ask for the money. Jeremy preferred to keep the friendship intact, not mixing affection with economics. He thought that friendship at the end should be a sentiment of affection instead of an exchange of economic favors or services.

Family relationships, on the other hand, are different, but they are also as good, or better than butterfly watching. However, there is a catch a metamorphosis may be on the way. Over time, family members may get transformed and become wasps instead. A family breakup is harder than a friendship breakup. You want to be careful, but you may be unlucky, the events unfold unexpectedly, you may have no control over the behavior of individuals. In a family breakup you get stung with some poison, and of course, it hurts. It is possible to recover from the stung, but there are additional risks, an allergic reaction can have long lasting effects. Family wounds cannot be easily healed and maybe never. An advantage is that the metamorphosis may backfire, and the wasps become butterflies again; hurt, hit, bruised and older, but butterflies anyway, to be enjoyed.

Family relationships are also related primarily to affective needs. However, there are responsibility and solidarity concerns that must be dealt with. The nuclear family, composed of parents and children requires strong responsibility bonds. Parents have to comply with the needs of children until they become adults. It is important to understand that human beings are born to be autonomous and once you are an adult you must be able to provide for yourself.

Solidarity is also required during those initial years. Once children grow up the responsibility and solidarity issues become mitigated, but use to remain available when needed. After the years, the solidarity can be applied both ways: including sons and daughters towards parents. Other members of the extended family, such as aunts, uncles and grandparents can have solidarity considerations toward their relatives, but not to the point to assume responsibilities that belong to the parents.

There is another type of relationship among people that is not precisely friendship, but that may look on the surface like it. It could be called 'interested acquaintances,' they look like a friendship but they are motivated by favors, services, or economic interest. This type of relationship promotes empathy and solidarity for the sole objective of getting a similar favor in the future. Somebody gives a ride to a neighbor and expects to get a ride back in the future. A mother asks a neighbor to take care of their children and expects to offer a similar favor in the future.

It should be understood that there are several levels of affection in friendships, family relationships, acquaintances, and known or unknown people around. It would be possible to affirm that affection is bigger with family, followed by friendship and in a lesser degree with acquaintances, known and unknown people. These levels of affection may have the variety provided by fuzzy logic, a mathematical approach where results are not binary or precise, and allows lots of variety. In those affective relationships, solidarity is the winner, people tend to apply solidarity must of the time, while responsibility happens just in the parents-children bond, while they are not adults. People do not like responsibilities, therefore let us take it easy.

SOCIALIST BINGO - Germinal Boloix

Jeremy remembered Renphys, a friend of his parents. Renphys told him once, "The last thing I wish is to lose your friendship because of differences in our political viewpoints about Small Venice. I had a similar discussion with a friend living in Algeria several years ago. We disagreed about the liberation of the country and our friendship collapsed."

Renphys and Jeremy disagreed about the new elected 'pseudo-socialistic' government in charge of Small Venice. Renphys was defending the regime and Jeremy was trying to convince him that it was a militaristic regime, with pseudo-socialistic tendencies, that was not going to improve the life of the people. Jeremy was not fond at all of a military winning the elections to impose a pseudo-socialist society with military support. Renphys believed socialism was a good alternative and he confronted Jeremy in every statement. The problem was that Renphys spoke like a Marxist considering the inevitability of socialism and communism without giving arguments in favor or against. Jeremy couldn't stand people in favor of a military-socialistic regime without arguments. The final touch came up when Jeremy said, "Go Spain!" during a Soccer World Cup and Renphys told him that it was the Spanish dictator's slogan; Jeremy hated the dictator, it was an insult for him. His friendship with Renphys came to an end some weeks later; Jeremy didn't email him anymore.

The breakup with Renphys is not the only one he remembers, there have been some other friends and family members involved in similar disputes. The problem usually starts with someone saying, "I am not interested in getting in trouble with you, I have enough problems in my life as to wish to break up with you." When Jeremy hears such words, he understands something is not going well and the next step is separation. Separating from friends has had no major impact in his life, but separation from family has had more severe consequences. Jeremy is relatively strong sentimentally, but he has suffered as any other human beings in those few occasions. The healing process makes you stronger.

Gabriel and Jeremy have kept in touch more or less during the years. However, when they started their own families lost contact. After about 10 to 15 years later, they started to meet again, not with their families tough. Jeremy remembers contacting Gabriel for a job teaching position at the College level, applied and got the job. During a conversation, Gabriel mentioned having problems of divorce, but Jeremy didn't try to find out more details. Jeremy knows how difficult is to be married; divorce is not a rare disease. In his last visit to the farm Gabriel showed what he had done;

basically growing trees, such as avocados, cocoa, plantains, and lately some Neem trees. He had cattle some time ago but abandoned for sanitary reasons.

Gabriel is the most philosopher friend Jeremy has had. Sometimes, Gabriel has said things like happiness or love does not exist. Jeremy uses to read about all these subjects and has his own opinion about them, answers sometimes with a joke. One time he told him about love, there is a song 'Non esiste l'amor' sang by Adriano Celentano, listen to it and tell me if you still feel the same or have changed your mind. About happiness suggested watching Daniel Gilbert's videos about the subject: Love, Music, Exercise, and Conversation. When things go your way, you feel happy, otherwise, you start saying happiness does not exist.

Today Jeremy asked Gabriel to come to Beach Town using public transportation because he has no car. When he arrived around noon, they went walking for lunch in one of the restaurants near the beach resort. Because the usual conversation in the country is related to the economic and political situation, Jeremy started saying that a socialist government is not viable. He had been reading books and articles in Internet and arguments are convincing, socialism has no future. Besides, over the years, Jeremy disapproves socialism or communism, it is not the solution for a society. Gabriel is a devil's advocate, even if he disagrees with something, he brings arguments in favor; it is his way of approaching conversations.

Gabriel was saying that socialism has been defined as a strategy in which the things we need to survive, work and control of our own lives—the industries, services and natural resources—are collectively owned by The People, and in which the democratic organization of The People within the industries and services is the government.

Gabriel never was an extrovert in favor of socialism, but that introduction made him look like one, using his powerful devil's advocate advantages, "I feel that socialism looks like the unique alternative to capitalism, that is the reason why is so popular."

"But socialism, as defined, goes against merit, it doesn't matter who you are or what you know. Everybody is equal, independently of their ignorance and contribution. Why is everybody going to own everything? Who is going to take care of things if they don't belong to anybody?"

As far as we know, continued Jeremy, the first two words any baby learns after being born are mama and mine. Mama or mom is very important for the child because her future depends on her mother. Mine is automatically learned, my bottle, my toy, my mom, my food, and so on.

SOCIALIST BINGO - Germinal Boloix

There is an instinctive desire to possess affection or something; people are born with that need to possess artifacts. Why socialists are going to say now that everything is collective, that a person is not allowed to own something.

Gabriel kept on going defending, "socialism tries to make people conscious of the needs of everybody, to have solidarity, to avoid egoism, to be helpful they must collaborate with each other."

One severe critique of socialism, said Jeremy, is their lack of innovation strategies. In socialism, the society gets stagnant because there is no major motivation to create better products or processes. Once basic needs like food distribution for all are accomplished, the socialist society doesn't struggle to keep improving.

Gabriel protested, "In capitalism, there is no motivation to collaborate with others nor solidarity."

"But listen, in a capitalistic society, it has been demonstrated that people may collaborate with each other too, without imposing any forced solidarity. Capitalism considers individuals and collectives at the same time. It allows individual and collective initiatives." Even though Jeremy is not defending capitalism, now he looked like the messenger of the Empire.

Looking like a socialist fanatic, Gabriel said, "The problems of capitalism are many: money, profit, richness, egoism, and so on."

"Imagine, the President is asking for an increase of petroleum prices forcing consumers to pay whatever he suggests, a purely authoritarian point of view. Besides, egoism is a natural phenomenon. Who socialists think they are to change human nature?"

In capitalism some amount of profit is required for research and development, socialists don't recognize these expenses because they don't promote innovation, represent a retrograded mentality, thought Jeremy.

"But you must agree that an ideology based on collaboration and people's participation is a strong force that attracts adepts, don't you think so?" Gabriel insisted.

"Yes, I understand why many people feel attracted to these ideas, but it doesn't imply that they are right. Nobody has demonstrated that the theory of socialism is correct."

"That happens under any circumstances, governments are made with people that follow rules, people are fallible and rules may be unclear," concluded Gabriel.

According to Jeremy, curiosity and invention require freedom, and he prefers freedom better than oppression. Freedom has more potential to produce better life than socialistic collective restrictions that produce misery.

"Listen Gabriel," continued Jeremy, "I believe that some people must be prepared for decision making and others for performing the decisions. Some decisions require wider knowledge, taking into consideration the surrounding context. Everybody cannot be involved in all decisions, it would mean a waste of time for society; nothing would be done."

Feeling like fish in water, Jeremy continued, "Knowledge spread out by socialists is a double edged razor blade, you plan to educate for a purpose and get the opposite result at the end. Let us take the case of sending people to the Island, to make them more socialistic, and most of the time they come back fully equipped against that type of regime."

In the latest Michael Moore's documentary, "Where to Invade Next," said Gabriel, in Germany workers have a big participation at the enterprise Directorate level. These workers are elected from the rank and file and they exchange with other managers. It seems the experience of workers' participation has been well appreciated because they give good feedback on decision making.

"Listen, you are talking about Germany, not precisely a socialist country," said Jeremy.

"Jeremy, you are getting me into much trouble, I am trying to be the devil's advocate and you do not let me with your convincing arguments."

Jeremy agreed on some degree of participation, but the chosen ones must be the best prepared, not anybody as is common practice in this socialist country. Besides, at the end some final decisions must be made that does not satisfy everybody, therefore negotiation is required. Worker participation is healthy, but do not forget that managers, engineers, and other professions are important to increase productivity, sometimes even more important than laborers. Jeremy presented his point of view about knowledge saying that in Orthodox Socialism there is a class viewpoint that makes them discriminative; knowledge is minimized in those countries. Socialists believe that knowledge and work are not important, only loyalty to the revolution is.

"I believe that you are on the right track, Jeremy. The weakness of laborers is evident, they lack knowledge, and socialists want to pull out its importance; they forget about the need of education, to favor merits and train them on new skills. Participation of workers is good, but merits must be part of the equation. Only technically capable workers must be allowed in the direction of enterprises and not precisely revolution's political fanatics."

Labor will always be sold, continued Jeremy, because workers need income to live and pay for their expenses; special cases of people incapable of working must be considered. Besides, socialists are creating a fictitious division among people, two classes, those that know and those that don't. Not because you are a manager or engineer you belong to a different class, you are a worker too. All your statements in favor of socialism demonstrate clearly that it is an invention that has never been realized; it is risky to get into improvisation and bother new generations with socialist regimes that have never demonstrated feasibility.

There is a video presenting Steve Jobs, the mastermind behind Apple Computers, talking about the importance of involving the best people on any scientific development, recalled Jeremy. It also applies to the society: involve the best on important matters; politicians alone are going to overthrow society.

As a good revolutionary, Gabriel replied, "You are mentioning one of the masterminds of new capitalism, Steve Jobs, the creator of smart phones and tablets, a clear representation of capitalism."

"A socialistic society wouldn't be able to create new technology; there are too many freedom's controls and limitations. Socialists tend to live in the past, promoting old ways of production that don't keep up with the population explosion," added Jeremy as a good technician.

Gabriel concluded on a better note, "I agree with you, some degree of innovation is required in our society. Stagnant approaches, such as socialism or Communism are not going to benefit humanity."

After a couple of hours of talking, Gabriel and Jeremy still had the time to eat some fish, fried plantain and drink a couple of beers.

"Listen, I must go. I have no car and it is difficult to find public transportation late in the afternoon. I must go buy a special irrigation hose for the farm in Claim-Town and I need still an hour or so to get there."

"Why do not you take a motorcycle taxi at the corner and they will take you fast to the highway, motorcycles use to come here frequently. I prefer to go walking to my house, even though the sun is strong and bad for my skin."

Gabriel said, "OK, see you next time. Please, figure it out how the capitalistic or socialistic strategy affects the life of people. I will be thinking about it myself."

"So long."

Reflecting on the conversation with Gabriel it is possible to understand why socialism is not a solution. A devil's advocate was not capable of sustaining the socialist approach therefore, socialism is not viable. Collectivities do not deserve to be superior to individuals.

Chapter 9: Marxism at The Institute

Jeremy has known Ursula for many years, is about ten years older than him. They knew each other because her parents came from Spain, and lived the same difficulties as Jeremy's parents. Ursula studied at the University and was graduated in Economy. When Jeremy visited tourist attractions around the country when he was young, went in an old car driven by his father. They used to camp with small tents while traveling; he remembers camping in the Andean road in front of the mountains and close to precipices. He clearly remembers Ursula, coming with them on some occasions. She is a smart lady and Jeremy appreciates her very much.

A sad anecdote about Ursula is that when she was young had a fiancée, but her father didn't let her marry because the groom was catholic and wanted to get married at the church. Her father had a strong opinion against the church and refused her wedding. Well, the point is that Ursula never married and has been living alone, let us say without a husband, for the rest of her life.

When Jeremy was a teenager, Ursula gave him a copy of Sacco and Vanzetti's book, two wrongfully executed workers that claimed anarchistic ideas. This was the first case of injustice committed in the world because of workers fighting for their rights. Jeremy read that book many years ago, he doesn't recall much of it, he knows the workers were not guilty but they were wrongly punished because of their affiliation with libertarian groups; it would be a matter of reading it a second time. Ursula is a good case of a person with socialistic and communistic ideas to be interviewed. Jeremy decided to give it a try to see how it goes.

She lives in a small apartment she bought with her parents; it is close to the Institute where she works. She has worked there all her life, he uses to do teaching and research. Jeremy invited her to talk close to her office and they met at a cafeteria nearby. The Institute is located in an old building owned by Jesuits. It has been rented for many years for educational purposes. The building has 4 quite tall stages, the stairs take a while to walk up; there are over 100 steps up to the last stage. Jeremy recalls going up many times because the elevator was damaged. At least, it was a good exercise to stay up in shape.

After taking the subway and close to the Institute Jeremy sent a text to Ursula and she came down. When they met, Jeremy gave her a strong hug, it was over thirty years since the last time they saw each other. Jeremy knew that the subject to be dealt with was not at all agreeable to Ursula she has remained loyal to lefties ideas all her life. They sat in the cafeteria and asked for coffee, with milk for Ursula and cappuccino for Jeremy. He started explaining that according to his experience, socialism was not a good regime to follow. He wanted to know in her own words how Ursula had evolved on her socialistic or communistic ideas.

She, as a good teacher, explained that Marx supported a theory of progress through economic conflict. Marx sustained that the surplus value created by the proletariat was the only source of profit. And it entailed exploitation, hence unavoidable conflict between the bourgeoisie and the proletariat. Because of repeated economic crisis and recessions, the working class would be aware that the system only benefits the minority; therefore the working class would rise up in revolution against capitalism. A transitional phase, where the majority proletarian class would rule, will determine the collective ownership of all industries and Communism would be achieved.

As you know quite well, said Jeremy, Marx wrote a book called The Capital, it repeats over and over the same arguments; it is a long book that requires lots of patience to assimilate. Marx identifies important subjects and gives a fair description, but he fails to present the whole picture of the problem. His bias toward laborers is almost comic; a society is made of politicians, magnates, bureaucrats, workers, managers, laborers, supervisors, professionals, aristocrats, idles, sicks, and so on. This bias towards laborers makes Marx's book a slim contribution.

She knows the history and said, "At the time, Marx's contribution was enormous. I still feel Marx gave depth to the social struggle. I have to recognize things have changed over the years but the struggle must continue."

Marx was biased toward the laborer, he only saw the exploitation by the capitalist, like a mother whose child is mistreated and protects him. Usually, mothers do not complain about their children misbehavior, they defend them even if they deserve punishment. Marx was not far away to think like a saving mother, he did not consider laborers being lazy, unproductive, or saboteurs, he put all of them as a whole, another idealized collective. This image reminded him immediately about the film Viridiana, directed by Luis Buñuel, where the lady tries to help some beggars and finds out at the end that they are a bunch of rascals that even try to rape and steal her; Marx is doing the same, he wants to protect workers blindly without noticing that there some that deserve and others that do not, the famous situation of willing to place everybody inside the same bag.

Jeremy has read the first 10 chapters of the Capital, and he was not impressed at all. Some people still believe that Marxism, going through socialism and communism, is the solution. Marx's work was directed to laborers, to get their support, it demonstrates he was a great strategist, was allied with the majority, the laborers, to become famous.

Ursula, being a good researcher, said, "There are new proposals around the globe complementing Marx's viewpoint, but they are not well studied yet. The Marxists fell asleep on their laurels."

He was explaining that he is not a fan of orthodox capitalism or 'wild capitalism,' he prefers a productive society, based on benefits derived from work, instead of pure financial profit.

She has known for many years how the rich think about their privileges and replied, "Listen, tell rich capitalists to abandon their good life and start working hard. Their answer is going to be, in your dreams!"

He also despises Orthodox Socialism or 'wild socialism,' where people get free money, subsidies, homes, appliances and food without major effort. People that support the party in power benefit from the government financial vault, full of petrodollars.

As a sensible woman, she said, "The idea is to help those that lack basic capabilities. But taking into consideration that there always are profiteers."

Jeremy is fond of merit; his motto is that you earn what you need according to your capacity, effort, and results. Nobody deserves more than what produces unless is sick. He thinks Marx can be admired for his contribution because he proposed an interpretation of the world considering human labor. However, failed to understand human nature, did not study what motivates human beings.

She is a big promoter of solidarity, she has gone to help directly in poor neighborhoods, spends many weekends visiting the needy and said, "Most people are born with basic capacities to prosper in life, but many others have lots of difficulties. Social systems are made to help the sufferers."

Life is not a struggle of poor against rich, said Jeremy, it requires empathy among people. Human nature requires earning your position through effort and merits, not over invented rights. A government by men and women of merit and honor is preferable than a government of popularity contests. Each man and woman must be recruited according to their abilities, avoiding incompetents. Honesty and merit define who should stay in government, not force or rigged elections.

Ursula recognized the truth of the statements and agreed, "Any social system should be based on merits, it's a built-in capacity of the human race. People react against those that don't contribute."

Nobody is capable of reading Karl Marx's Capital book, but Jeremy suggested anyway, "If there is something wrong with socialism, it has to be there, in his book."

She explained, "Marx was some kind of hero at the time of his book and many people followed his vision. The word Marxism has a popular meaning that people enjoy. However, the book is not about socialism is against capitalism."

Marx gave a contribution to the working class, by suggesting commodity value came from labor. This is a remarkable contribution, but after 1848, many changes in the society have been introduced, for example Agricultural, Industrial, Technological, and Communicational.

She believes in progress and understands current contributions, and finally said, "Of course, the society needs new approaches, to make explanations of a new society according to the modern world. I hope our society is not going be retrograded 200 years as some religions propose."

Labor needs different levels of knowledge, said Jeremy, and Marx didn't clarify it at the time, he was obsessed with laborers. Marx made the difference between use value and exchange value, but only in terms of labor, he did not identify the context where such commodities were offered: the market is always there, if people do not buy, products are worth nothing.

Using her skills as a good researcher she said, "An analysis considering human nature and modern societies could be recommended to produce a new order of ideas that contribute to a better society."

Marx talked about private proprietors, said Jeremy, and placed them as owners of commodities, and he also talked about the market where commodities are exchanged. Marx introduced the notion of money, trying to find the universal equivalent. Money is the manifestation of the value of commodities. Of course, beneath money, all is components and labor, but machinery cannot be forgotten. Marx introduced the notion of the utility of an object for consumption and the utility for the purpose of exchange. Gold and silver were suggested as possible universal exchange commodities; the society becomes one of commodity producers. He introduced non-commodities such as conscience and honor, capable of being offered for sale by their holders; acquiring through price, the form of commodities. It is an object with a price without having value (labor value).

Marx talks about the metamorphosis of commodities: a commodity is transformed into a use-value artifact; the money commodity starts to take shape. Commodities express their prices in gold, the money-form. Marx presented the C-M-C (Commodity-Money-Commodity) regular cycle: somebody produces a commodity, sells it and buys another commodity. For the commodity-owner is a sale; for the money-owner is a purchase. The next notion is Alienation when somebody sells his labor. Circulation of commodities sweats money from every pore. The values of commodities remaining constant, their prices vary with the value of gold. This is known as the currency of money.

She continued explaining: Marx talks about a metamorphosis being interrupted, money ceases to be mobilized; it changes from 'meuble' to 'immeuble.' Sellers become hoarders of money doing sales without purchases. Money is the means of payment. Universal money is silver and gold; there are some other money representations, such as bills and plastic, allowed to circulate.

Marx introduced the Transformation of Money into Capital: instead of C-M-C, M-C-M (buying in order to sell) starts to appear, it is M-M at the end, to make monetary profits. C-M-C is use-value oriented, while M-C-M is exchange-value oriented.

She continued on surplus value coming up with a profit, the expansion converts it into capital. Money as capital is an end in itself, the circulation of capital has no limits; money adds value to itself changes and expands. It represents money that is worth more money. M-C-M is the formula for Capital.

All this discussion about capitalism is clear, said Jeremy, looking only for financial profits is counterproductive for the society. Capitalism has its negative aspects that must be corrected, but it does not mean that socialism is going to solve the progress of the people. He kept going, if collective enterprises, own by the workers, were productive, they would be already part of any democratic government. If they are not popular is because they don't respond to the needs of people. The only examples of collectively owned enterprises in a democracy are the stock market (a capitalist invention), that we already know has many arguments against, Clubs where members pay for capital and maintenance purposes, and non governmental organizations non profit oriented.

Ursula said surprisingly, "I agree with you in this case because Absurd Socialism was incapable of building a productive society, they have only produced parasites."

The big mistake, according to Jeremy, is to believe that the society must be run under a unique model such as socialism, capitalism or communism. People in charge of defining policies must make up their minds and understand that society must function using the appropriate model according to social needs at the lower levels. It is unacceptable to run a country top down with Socialist ideas; it is too harsh on individuals. Let us take, for example, health care or education, should they function under a specific political strategy or a mix of approaches? Democracy must allow a mix of approaches, some socialists others capitalists. Forcing people to accept bad approaches is immoral; if a socialistic economy is not productive, it must be substituted by a capitalistic one.

She seemed to understand Jeremy's criticisms and said, "I have seen so many lost opportunities with this Absurd Socialism that I almost agree with you."

He tried to send a message about his approach, saying that he wanted to study socialism from a scientific point of view. He said that his opinions were not capricious; it was not because he was stubborn or something similar to that. He wanted to make clear that he promoted a scientific study of political approaches that does not leave any doubts. He wanted to demonstrate that socialism was not viable. It can be done using different resources, including economy, mathematics, psychology, human relations, and many other experiences people may bring on to the discussion.

Communist Manifesto

Marx and Engels proposed the Communist Manifesto, said Ursula, one hundred and sixty-eight years ago. It proposed a series of actions to transform a country: abolition of the property of land, getting rent from land for public purposes, keep a progressive income tax, abolition of inheritance, confiscation of property, centralization of credit by means of a national bank, State centralization of communication and transport, assign the State land and factory production, force everybody to work in the land and factories, distribute the population over the country, and provide free education.

Is it possible to demonstrate, asked Jeremy that all these measures are going to produce a better society? To me there is no way to demonstrate its success; therefore, they are just wishes or fantasies of those interested in power. It is a way of looking different for purposes of gaining popularity and getting votes on elections. It is a way of lying to the people and looking important. It is their way of using democracy as a mechanism to rise to power, controlling the countries of the world without solving the real issues of justice, freedom and prosperity.

Analyzing each of the actions of the Communist Manifesto, thought Jeremy, it is possible to notice that they contain an important message: improve on justice for all, not just for some. All the population needs justice and opportunities, it is not only for those in power or with money everybody needs it: rich or poor, important or common, black or white, men or women.

The world evolved conquering territories, the land was confiscated by usurpers, those that took land wrongfully and stayed in power by force, said Ursula.

But there is a chain of proprietors of land that didn't invade territories, they simply bought the land later on from the State, continued Jeremy; are they in fault by buying the land? Or is the State in fault for selling the land? We need more inventive solutions to make justice, not simply taking the land away from owners. Isn't there enough land available to produce the goods people need? If the answer is negative, something should be done to recover the land and make it productive. If the answer is affirmative, why do we worry about? there is enough land for all.

Ursula and Jeremy kept talking about the points brought up in the Communist Manifest. It was Jeremy the one doubting about its validity. The Manifest is Utopian, it looks for a social justice at the expense of those that had the chance to own certain goods. Human evolution and society evolution should not be destroyed through a decree born from envy. The Manifest is pure envy, "if we cannot have what you own, then nobody can." The Manifest is violence, force some to yield their goods to please the envy of a population greedy for injustice. The justice of the poor is envy, why are you going to have things and I cannot have them?

Abolition of inheritance is a topic related to land ownership, parents passing their property to their children or relatives. Jeremy asked what justice abolition of inheritance brings in? Why must properties go to the State? Why must the State administrate properties and become so rich? Why is the State going to be a better administrator of a property than a relative? Why must decisions be so drastic, applying the same rule to all? Why must everybody be penalized the same way? Would not it be better to select what is justified and what it is not?

Jeremy did not inherit any material goods from his parents, everything he possessed was earned working during his life. He does not approve parents working like donkeys to give some inheritance to their kids. He only agrees with accumulating some goods to guaranty a sustainable old age and live a little better comfortably during life. Accumulating just for fun or to leave something to the kids should not be an objective. Children must be autonomous, do the same Jeremy did, earn a living and possess whatever you need for your old age and a better life. If by any chance you had a better opportunity and earned more than what you need, do the arrangements on time to distribute it among family members or charitable organizations you trust, the State does not deserve any gift, they are a bunch of thieves.

Confiscation of property is another measure that is in question, said Jeremy, why do we need to confiscate? Why do we need to confiscate everything? Why is the State a better administrator than private enterprises? Here we need some reasonableness, what is not well administered, or not providing the services people require, can begin a State requested confiscation procedure. But if the property is well administered and provides the required services, there is no way to justify confiscation.

Centralization of Bank credit is another case that must be analyzed. Why does the State wants to control all the banks? Why does the State believes it knows how to use private funds? Why doesn't the State distribute instead the responsibilities and takes only those that allow it to stabilize the economy, such that there are no recession surprises over time? The problem is always the same, the State believes it deserves decision making on all areas. It is better to establish percentages of credit distribution taking in consideration some variety in the population.

Ursula was listening, she understood all these measures in the manifest were against freedom and she was not retrograde. She followed Jeremy's remarks attentively without interfering much on his explanations.

Communication and transport centralization by the State are similar to the case of banks, said Jeremy. Why must the State do everything? Isn't enough to participate controlling what is done without doing it themselves? The State may contract works in this domain and keep some areas for execution and let others to free enterprises.

Land and factory ownership by the State is also unwelcome he said. Why does the State believes in its capability to administer the whole land of a country? Who has said that a monster like the State is performing better than private enterprises? The State must be satisfied controlling the land and the economy from a high level, and not as an administrator and producer of all the goods and services. She intervened this time saying that capitalists use to buy land just to wait for increases in prices and without making it productive. Jeremy said that he agreed on intervention of the government when it is justified.

Free education sounds so nice, but we have to remember that education costs a lot, said Jeremy. Who is going to pay for it? Where is the government going to find the money to pay for education? It is better to find another way of helping the needy, by giving fellowships, instead of thinking that education is free. Fellowships have been around for so many years, it means they help those that deserve them. Ursula with her university experience agreed totally, saying that education needs investments and governments are not the best providers of capital.

We all know that any task requires different levels of knowledge, and Marx didn't clarify it at the time; Marx made the difference between use value and exchange value, but only in terms of laborers, he didn't identify the context where such commodities were offered; for example, the investment to build the factories, the equipments, the tools, the supplies needed. Additionally, the market was always there, independently of what name you wanted to give to it; if the buying capacity is low, nobody can buy.

After talking so much about politics, Jeremy felt extenuated. Ursula was listening to him all the way, although she was not convinced about his opinions of the Manifesto. Ursula has been involved for many years in this type of discussion and she believes that there is not a definitive answer about those critiques. Jeremy agreed by saying that the Manifesto was written so many years ago and that it contains old ideas that must be updated. Ursula had to return to her office and she hugged Jeremy and said "Au revoir."

Reflecting on the conversation with Ursula it is possible to establish that Marxism has a strong influence on socialism. The unique contribution of Marx was to speak in the name of workers, nothing else. Human nature is not discussed, Marxism tries to change people into an idealistic machine; and we know humans are born with intrinsic defects, therefore the political system is incapable of changing humans. Do not force injustice by introducing wrong political regimes.

Chapter 10: Green Tablecloth Restaurant

Jeremy appreciates very much his friend Ivory they met for the first time at the University when hippies were famous. Ivory is a natural born hippie, a nice guy, easy to talk and exchange, he seems to love everybody and most people love him. Jeremy went partying with him many times, fetching him to parties and taking him back home. At the time, Jeremy had an old 1995 Dodge car, it was called the 'blue bird,' later on he owned an old DKW jeep. One night, going to a party, he was stopped on a highway because it was not allowed to drive a jeep without a roof and full of people. He remembers somebody on the back of the jeep talking to the policeman and finally convincing him to let us exit the highway, explaining that we were going to a party, and so on.

As any normal man, Jeremy was very interested in ladies, in fact, all he met at school and parties looked attractive to him. But because of his studies, he didn't establish a permanent relationship with any. On the other hand, he didn't like to spend much time after girls, that endeavor takes too much time, he had to finish his career first, to graduate was his main objective. Jeremy had a few girlfriends before marrying, he met one at a party with other students, including Ivory's cousin; that relationship didn't last long, probably for the best. The girl, without a valid reason, menaced to denounce him with her father that worked for the local criminal police department. Because of a few hugs, some blunt kisses, and some rubbing here and there, the woman menaced him unjustly; Jeremy forgot about her quite easily. This girlfriend had a sister that married Ivory later on in his life.

Jeremy has been always intrigued about marriage, why people get married, without understanding what it means and what the difficulties are? Marriage contains the most important aspects of being happy. According to Daniel Gilbert, happiness involves love, music, exercise, and chat. In a marriage is easy to find sex and chat because there are two individuals involved. Sex involves some exercise but is not enough to keep you fitted, you need to do some additional exercise. Music can be found buying some records and play some music. Do not expect your spouse to be a Diva.

Another explanation he found about marriage, besides love and company, was that people know their parents were married and that they had an apparently healthy relationship, why yours is going to fail? Marriage is a difficult endeavor; people shouldn't get involved unless they have analyzed all the consequences. To get along in a marriage, the 50% rule does not work, only the 100% rule applies. If both disagree, there is no solution, there is stagnation.

Extremes are wrong and finding too many problems on marriage issues is not convenient either. But being too soft and uncaring is a bad approach, take marriage seriously. Better make early decisions, quit or stay, than wait to the last minute. Jeremy recalls the case of a neighbor that never married, she used to find problems with all her boyfriends; at the end, she was the lover of a married man, she never married or had children.

A severe distortion in a marriage happens when one of the members has obvious defects. It is typical to say that he or she is going to change in the future, that we are going to help her. For example, if he has problems of bad character, laziness, violence, drugs, or did not study while young; the partner says he is going to change in the future. The mistake is that people cannot change as her partner needs, it is impossible, therefore it is better to consider separation on time instead of insisting on becoming social workers. If you accept your partner as he is, you are going to suffer consequences, do not expect miracles. It is a problem of human nature, we are like that, we were born with some characteristics, difficult or impossible to change.

His mind returned to his actual interests, games and society. Games are a universal part of the human experience, for all cultures, genders, and ages. He has been surrounded by games all his life, he remembers playing Marbles, Spinning Top, Cops and Robbers, Ludo, Monopoly, Checkers, and Chess. He loved games very much, he recalls watching a carousel her mother bought to give as a gift to another kid. He watched the carousel every day, on top of a drawer, before it disappeared in Christmas. Also, playing in his neighborhood a 'caimanera,' a bunch of kids after the ball, one day there was so much dirt powder that he could not see the ball at all.

Jeremy remembers his father teaching him to play Chess. He said, "Beware of Shepherd's Mate, you can lose the game in the first three or four moves." Jeremy played several times with his father when he was 10 years old. He would never forget the first time he beat his father, he was a teenager. He remembers reviewing and studying some chess magazines and going through complete matches by some masters. He started to understand better the game through his own effort. His father didn't say a word when he lost. Never more! it was the last match with him ever.

Jeremy didn't ask him to play again either. His father didn't spend time studying whereas he studied the game deeply.

In the same way as Jeremy played when he was a kid, he usually plays with his grandkids, and he enjoys it the same. They play dominoes, checkers, chess, cards, and sports. Through games, people interact and start to understand behavioral rules. Some kids have a better understanding of the importance of rules, while others have more difficulty and start inventing their own rules. Inventing new rules for a game is not absolutely bad; it is a way of inventing new approaches.

Because Jeremy usually beats his grandchildren on checkers and chess, he started to think in ways of encouraging them, giving some advantages. For example, in checkers, if you let one player make many free moves at the beginning, while the other does not move, does not give much of an advantage, the game is not sensible to that supposed advantage. "Now," thought Jeremy, "If I give my grandkid the advantage of taking one, two or three pieces before starting the game, is going to have a numeric advantage and would be able to beat me." It was a new way of looking at the game, using handicap advantages to those that play less, besides it nourishes research.

He recalls a modified chess game where there were two queens instead of one. The Professor who invented the new game was his fellow collaborator during a postdoctoral season many years ago. The professor was proud of inventing a new game with a 9X9 board and two queens. Jeremy's grandkids have already invented dozens of new ways of moving the pieces of chess around. In checkers, his grandkids have invented several moves jumping all over the pieces and turning at corners back and forth.

Most games involve competition, few may introduce collaboration. Many games are played individually; some accept groups cooperating to accomplish some goals. Key components of games are goals, rules, challenge, and interactivity. Rules represent the established framework for justice; when rules are not obeyed, it is difficult to agree on results.

Games generally involve mental or physical stimulation, and sometimes both. Many games are primarily mental, such as chess, others are physical such as any sport. Many games help develop practical skills, serve as a form of exercise, or an educational, simulation and psychological role. Games are useful to increase our intellectual and physical potential using our recreational time.

In any sport, the objective is to win, to practice a sport, have a good time, improve your health, amuse the fans, bring out families to cheer for us, or to feel good after the exercise. The definite objective is to compete and win. Any sport has health benefits, players are going to live better, feel better. Board games are also positives for human beings, some amusement is required once in a while. However, independently of the approach, socialistic or capitalistic, the objective of the game is well known, to win.

Because games represent a model of competition, it lets many people down, those that lose. Any game that is invented to produce winners and losers is a system that lets some people down.

Many people, thought Jeremy, have opined about my Game-Socialism approach, "It is the first time we hear somebody trying to use games for the purpose of analyzing a Society. We have our doubts, but we wish you luck on your endeavor. Jeremy, it is better to try and fail than never intend."

He answers clarifying, "I know there are some limitations, but I wish to demonstrate the effect of wrong policies applied to the game and that also happen in a real society."

Other people opined, "The concept of production in a Society is important, it means that goods and services must be generated to help citizens. In a game, sport or pastime, there are players acting on the field or the board, according to the rules and the random events allowed in the game. In a game, there is not a production notion unless it is simulated or abstract."

He used to say, "I guess most games may include a few of those terms used in the society. Games are usually associated with recreation; use to emphasize competition and winning, to beat the opponent. Board games can simulate a society but sports cannot."

And he continues justifying, "However, in most games, there are important notions about rules and justice. Any game has some rules to define its purpose and scope. Notions of justice establish the conditions to win. In all sports, there are referees to help interpret the rules and make decisions on the occurring events."

Jeremy was thinking aloud, is there a society game out there that simulates a cooperative economy, one that doesn't produce losers but winners instead? One that would not require you to prey off your neighbor (like Monopoly), or neglect your neighbor (like Gazdálkodj Okosan, a socialist game), but one in which there is an active collaboration to enhance the wealth of all. He was imagining a game that would illustrate the type of competition envisioned by Adam Smith that fosters not annihilation — but innovation, adaptation, and diversification.

He believed in a game that would also illustrate the social and economic benefits of employee and owners, of small, nimble and locally-rooted enterprises, of long-term resource stewardship and conservation. He could envision tournaments, where groups of players, wheeling, and dealing among themselves, seek to produce the greatest cumulative wealth for their team and the other groups. That is the sort of game that our national economies should be modeling.

He decided to visit his friend Ivory and spend some time talking about that idea: How can games be related to politics and how can they help understand a society? Do socialism and capitalism politics make a difference applied on games? He phoned Ivory and they decided to meet at the Green Tablecloths Restaurant. This was a popular and inexpensive Italian restaurant located in east downtown, in the center of the capital. They used to go there for lunch during many years until Jeremy found out that Ivory was a supporter of the new socialist regime. Jeremy didn't appreciate very much his sympathy for the regime but he couldn't do much to change his mind. Jeremy preferred to lose contact with Ivory instead of getting into an argument and possibly insult him; things were getting tough at the time because of politics.

He tried not to get in trouble this time and approached the conversation talking about philosophy instead of socialism. Jeremy was going to present his idea without mentioning the word socialism, he would use the term Society in general.

"Hello Ivory, how are you doing? Long time no see. When was the last time we met?"

"At least 15 years, remember? Since you found out about my sympathy for the Devil, I mean, for the leader of the revolution."

He changed the conversation, "Years are not passing by as the Oscar Wilde's Dorian Grey personage that never grew old. You have changed a lot in 15 years, isn't it?" Jeremy thought, Ivory is getting old fast, but why?

"That is true, I know I have changed, I watch myself every day in the mirror and I don't like what I see. By the way, you have changed a lot too. Did you say you want to talk about philosophy?" Asked Ivory.

He answered fast, to keep the conversation focused, "Yes, I am doing some informal research about games and society, precisely, how analyzing certain games can help me understand society."

SOCIALIST BINGO - Germinal Boloix

They checked the menu and ordered some soup for a starter and spaghetti with meatballs as a second plate. While waiting, Jeremy started saying that life can be considered a game and people must play it, there is no choice. People know that in life nothing is going to be won at the end because death is the last reward. The only way to quit the game of life is by dying; but while you are alive you must keep going.

"It seems to me that you are a bit harsh on yourself; I don't appreciate the emphasis on dying. To die is something that usually happens at the end of our life when we are old; therefore give me some other incentives to keep fighting and playing the game of life." Demanded Ivory.

"Ok Ivory, let us emphasize life instead of death, let us analyze the rules and the objectives of life, for the game of life, in a society."

"First of all, life is not like any game such as Monopoly, Soccer, Chess, Dominoes or Pokemon Go. Life has no precise rules, life has sidetracks and times when no specific objective is pursued." Being the first time they talked about the subject, Ivory seemed an expert.

"I would say that our conversation should be limited to find out some analogies between life and games and how games can be useful to understand society." Jeremy brought up his best arguments trying to palliate the misunderstanding.

The soup was arriving, was an Italian minestrone soup with lots of vegetables and beans. The soup was very hot; Jeremy had to pause, blowing to make it colder.

Jeremy continued the talking, "It is better to take life as a game instead of enduring suffering; however, most of the time life must be taken as hard as it is. It would be nice to play life enjoying it, without suffering much."

"But humans are not like that, they use to suffer more than enjoy, emotions and sentiments flowering out. Those that enjoy life too much, without suffering, are known as a sociopath, people without empathy for others and no fear of failure. They are prone to conflict and confrontation, their life may be chaotic, vicious and many times short."

"That is fine, better don't take life too seriously, but don't forget that you must take responsibility for your actions: don't do to others what you don't appreciate being done to you!"

The soup was excellent; Jeremy added some spicy sauce that improved the flavor. A soup gets a special flavor with a hot sauce and adding some avocado chunks makes it unbelievable, the flavors complementing each other.

Ivory also appreciated the quality of the soup, "The chef of the restaurant deserves a compliment, let us them know how good the soup was."

Going back to the subject, Jeremy said, "I would say that our conclusion is that life is not a game, but there are some aspects of life that make it resemble a game. In life, it is important to learn to win and to lose. Every day, people have good and bad experiences, equivalent to winning and losing in a game. Let me suggest another aspect, social games can be useful in understanding Society because people interact and follow the rules."

His friend had some insights, "I would say that a social game such as Monopoly is a model of a Society, but it represents only certain aspects of reality, for example, capitalism. Sports like baseball, football or soccer, have some rules, players, captains, technical directors, referees, locations and fans, and are limited by space and time constraints. Sports have a clear benefit, to improve the health of players and amuse the fans. Games have as its main objective to win the game, to compete and find out who is the best."

In life there are many objectives, continued Jeremy, winning is just one of them; there are as many objectives as people in the world. In life people play once, the time span is their whole life, unless you consider each day a new game.

Ivory added, "I would say that in life each day represents a new game, but we cannot forget the past, whatever we did affects our future. In life, our history has some weight that produces consequences, while in a game history does not count so much. The rules in a sport are known and interpreted by referees; therefore referees' opinions give some flexibility. In life, there are no precise rules; laws, norms, and regulations have some degree of imprecision. In a Society, the judicial system is the interpreter of laws and regulations and the governmental executive is in charge of managing the country. In a sport, the referee is the interpreter of the events and the captain and Technical Director are in charge of management."

"I like your inside it means is fruitful to use sports and board games as models to interpret society. Additionally, it would be possible to design a game of a society where Socialist and Capitalist approaches get demonstrated" said Jeremy, trying to motivate Ivory.

The spaghetti Neapolitan with meatballs arrived on time, Jeremy asked for a napkin to protect his shirt, he used to get sauce all over when eating spaghetti. Ivory took a tablespoon and a fork to eat his spaghetti, said he learned it when he went to Italy 30 years ago, just after graduating from school.

Jeremy recalls that time, he went visit Ivory and found out that he was gone on a trip. Why Ivory didn't say a thing, he left without a trace. Her mother said that he left without explanation, "I am happy that he is OK, he phoned and said he was doing well, it seems he is doing some simple jobs such as taking care of dogs in the neighborhood, he gets paid by the hour."

Showing his eyeballs, Jeremy asked her, "Do you have any idea when is he coming back?"

"I don't, but as soon as he writes or phones, I'll let you know."

That was Ivory, unpredictable, hiding many secrets, without sharing with anybody. However, Jeremy remembers when Ivory asked him about having a relationship with a divorced with 3 kids, "Do you think it is a good idea to get involved in that relationship?"

"Well, if you love each other, why not?" said Jeremy at the time.

He finally married the lady and after a few years and one or two more children, Ivory divorced. Today, Jeremy would have given him a different advice. His experiences in life taught him otherwise: don't get involved in complex relationships, simplify as much as you can.

His friend worked for many years as an engineer, and later on earned good money doing government contracts, he got rich working for the new socialist regime. Now as a mature man, Ivory confesses himself being a communist, "I am going to stamp my vote on top of the little red cock that represents the communist party in the country." Why didn't he confess before, when he was young? Thought Jeremy and watched Ivory while thinking about old times, when he was young and spoke about Anarchism instead of Communism, but Ivory never showed himself off as a communist.

Ivory, that did not know what Jeremy was thinking in that precise instant said, "Listen if you are looking for games to model society, why don't you take Monopoly: buy real estate and utilities, build an empire and earn lots of money. I still keep some Monopoly bills somewhere."

Manage your Finances Wisely

This is another socialist game invented in Hungary that simulates people living in socialism. It is called 'Gazdálkodj Okosan' in Hungarian. It is similar to Monopoly but oriented to a socialist society. 'Go' is the factory where the competing proletarians work. Every time you land on or pass it, it is payday. 'Wheel of Fortune' cards perform the function of chance and community chests. There are also spaces designated for the butcher, the restaurant, the zoo, the shoe shop, the nightclub - and tellingly, right after payday - the liquor store.

The aim of the game, in proper socialist fashion, is *not* to amass an empire of property and wealth. The objective is to buy an apartment and furnish it. The one who does is first wins the game. People get their salaries each time they go around the board; they pay for the apartment and pay to buy furniture. People can spend their salaries also paying for food, restaurant, going to the movies, and going to sport events. The game discourages buying alcohol or tobacco. Players cannot trade their furniture with other players to avoid black market speculation.

The board game, besides Ludo, that Jeremy has played the most was Monopoly, he felt emotional and said, "When I was a teenager, I used to play lots of Monopoly, buying all the properties in a street, then houses and finally hotels, and getting rich charging rent and getting income. It was amusing to me, getting so much fake money."

His friend showing off his hidden communist ideals said, "Why do you think you are against socialism? You played Monopoly too much!"

Jeremy did not agree at all with the comment and tried to explain, "I would say that it was just a game, nobody becomes capitalist or communist because of a game. It is the same case as visiting the Island, you are not going to become a communist because of strolling Havana, or going to 'La Bodeguita del Medio,' or plunging into a beach in the Island. You may instead repudiate the Society of the Island when you get a chance to know their sufferings."

Ivory, influenced by his stubborn communist beliefs, defended the need to progress toward socialism and communism.

A bit perturbed emotionally for this retrograde view and changing the subject, Jeremy added, "By the way, have you heard of any game that presents socialist strategies. I guess socialists, with their old viewpoints, have not even been capable of inventing a game to promote their ideas."

"There is a game called Kolejka, invented in Poland, it simulates the life during the Cold War in Communist Poland several years ago. I am not proud of that game by the way. It is a critique of Communism."

Kolejka

The board game *Kolejka* (a.k.a. Queue) tells a story of everyday life in Poland at the tail-end of the Communist era. The players' task appears to be simple: they have to send their family members out to various stores

SOCIALIST BINGO - Germinal Boloix

on the game board to buy all the items on their shopping list. The problem is, however, that the shelves in the five neighborhood stores are empty. Kolejka simulates people in lines to buy food, furniture, and other products. The game is played by two to five players, each controlling five pawns, representing their family members. Each family needs to do some shopping for events of any type such as birthdays or holidays, however, each player faces the problem of a shortage of needed goods.

The players have to decide which store to line up in front of, and can play various event cards such as 'This isn't your place,' 'Colleague in the government,' or 'Store closed,' changing the order of the pawns in the queue (which represents jumping the queue, or forcing other players out of it).

Jeremy already knew about the game and said, "This reminds me of Small Venice, suffering so much with scarcity. People in lines did not find basic products at regulated prices. People must cross the border, to our Brother Republic, to bring essential products to their families. There are 'Bachaqueros,' or big ants devourers, that buy to resell in the black market."

His friend was defending his ideas and said, "This 'Queue' game is a bad representation of socialism and communism; it is just propaganda against the revolutionary government of The People."

"Oh yeah, right, you always find an excuse in favor of socialist regimes."

Starting to become more and more defensive, Ivory continued, "The revolution must be done on the streets, not in a game. Long live the working class, power to laborers to control the government and the factories!"

Jeremy started to notice emotionality in his friend's red face and didn't want to get in trouble again because of politics. He changed the subject and added, there is another socialist game that simulates people living in socialism.

Getting calmer, Ivory tried to be pleasant, "It is interesting to know that a socialistic game is available, I guess it is not very popular in the world. Imperialism crushes the popularity of these games to avoid socialism in the world. Do you think it is a joke?"

"It is interesting to find out that some games have a socialist viewpoint, they could make the 'revolution' through games instead of against the people. A game hurts nobody." Said Jeremy emphasizing the harm socialism has done in Small Venice.

Ivory said, "Don't be so harsh on socialism, it is the only viable alternative the poor have, nobody is going to help them in capitalism, only socialism and communism will improve those in need."

"Not even in your dreams! Socialism has not demonstrated its viability, only the poor and ignorant can believe in a system that doesn't work, even its theory is faulty."

"Listen, up to now, only capitalism and socialism are the alternatives in the modern world, I still consider socialism superior to capitalism" stated Ivory trying to wrap things up.

Jeremy tried to be objective in his arguments and explained that he didn't agree with 'wild capitalism,' the one that only promotes financial profits without production. He didn't agree with 'wild socialism' either, the one that promotes discrimination by neglecting ideas and favoring only supporters of the regime, giving away money, gifts, food, supplies, appliances, and properties, including houses.

Although Jeremy was not planning to meet Ivory in the near future, he said, "Ivory, it was my pleasure to meet you again, I wish to see you shortly. It was a productive conversation. I guess I am going to be documenting our conversation in the future. Let us get together at a later time to review our conclusions about games and society."

Ivory has plenty of good feelings about Jeremy and said, "I'll be ready to meet with you anytime."

Chapter 11: Bingo at Beach Town

The next visit to Beach Town, Jeremy was in the house and got up early, he was lucky to have electricity to prepare some coffee with his electrical coffee maker; he still had some coffee left, he brought it from the capital, two half a kilo bags, one for her neighbor and one for him. In the town is difficult to find coffee, when it arrives gets sold fairly fast. He started to drink an early cup of coffee on the porch, watching the street and the houses in front, the houses' fences and the hanging power cables, and a few palm trees in the background; the morning blue sky gives some expectation of having a good hot day. It was March and there was a little wind improving the temperature. He remembered August as one of the hottest months, those months he felt his lungs getting cook at noon.

That morning, Jeremy went to buy some groceries, he found his friend Palmira a few blocks ahead and started to talk to her, "Good morning, how is everything? How is your kid?"

"Everything is OK, my son is still sleeping, he has a cold and needs some rest. If you need to buy eggs, go to the Chinese Market, they still have some. You know how difficult is to find some food these days."

"What happens is that we do not find what we need. I would pay a higher price for regulated food," said Jeremy.

"I understand, but if things are more expensive, we will not be capable to pay for them. By the way, do you want to play bingo tonight? We get together most nights and some weekends."

"Yes, of course, I'll try to go play bingo, thanks. The evenings I have not much to do, I don't like the TV programs and I have only one channel available; they present mostly soap operas and Miss Universe contest."

These years have had an increase in Bingo gaming in town, families get together to play bingo more often than before. Neighbors get together in big groups so that bingo prizes are bigger, sometimes they meet during the week and other times during the weekend. On weekdays they use to play after 8 pm, and during weekends they play after 4 pm.

Bingo is a well known social game, it has to be highlighted the importance of the relationship among players. Jeremy was inspired by those relationships within an informal set up of the game, he was able to propose a new approach to define the relations in a society. It is important to stress that in a formal set up of the game was not possible to get inspired. In a formal set up, people sit down quiet waiting for the next number to be called, there is no opportunity of exchange with other players. In an informal bingo set up, it is possible to talk to other players, have some exchanges and watch the gestures of other players.

One or two years ago, Jeremy was invited to play and he sat down around a table, people had been there for one or two hours already. He got a card and some little stones to mark his card. He started to notice that one of the players was winning most of the games, calling always 'bingo'; there was not any major checking to verify the numbers. The games that night was very fast, after just ten or fifteen balls were drawn, there was a winner. It is not normal to complete patterns so fast, it usually takes 30 or more balls. Jeremy didn't win a game the whole night. He was not impressed by his lack of success and never went back to play.

Tonight Palmira welcomed him, seemed happy to see him, there were about ten players around the table. He took a chair and sat beside the light, to be able to see his numbers clearly. He chose a card and played that night without luck; he tried to pay attention to the more frequent numbers anyway. The set up was quite informal, the balls were drawn one by one; the drawer used them to mark her own card. When somebody called bingo, there was an attempt to check the winning card without much effort. Because it was his first time playing, he couldn't give any precise feedback, but he was not a happy loser. Each game cost only 10 Pesos per card. He lost around 300 Pesos that night; it is not really much these inflationary days, it is much less than an American dollar, but still is a losing streak, around 15 games lost with two cards per game.

The next day, thinking about his first Bingo experience, he remarked that the players kept the same cards for every game. They were playing with the same card all the time, it seems some people even took their cards home. Any organized Bingo reunion requires new cards distributed randomly every game. Jeremy didn't know about how they selected their cards, it seemed they choose a card that gave them some winning games. It meant they noticed that some numbers were more frequent than others. Jeremy also tried to identify which were the most common numbers being drawn: 17, 46, 75, 21, 8, and 34.

Next time I am going to choose a better card, with most of the numbers that appear more often thought Jeremy. The next day, Palmira told him to choose one card and start playing, he decided to choose winning cards. That night, he lost at least 400 Pesos more, the cards were better than before but it was not enough to make him a winner.

The next day, after buying some supplies, Jeremy saw Palmira outside her house and said, "I suggest the organizers let newcomers win at least one game, such that they get motivated and keep playing." Palmira didn't answer, meaning she didn't understand how to let somebody win a game. Jeremy knew there was not precisely a rigged bingo, but people were submissive to the practices imposed by Palmira to choose the cards.

Later, when Jeremy saw Marbella, said, "Human beings are very smart, when playing they pay attention to the most frequent numbers."

"No, I think it is a matter of luck, it is not because of any frequency count."

He insisted, "Intelligence, among other things, is associated with logic, learning, and memory. It's an innate capacity; people don't need to make a big effort to use it in daily life."

"I don't understand how counting frequent numbers is going to help me win games," she answered a bit innocent.

Jeremy knows about probability theory and said, "Tell me why you keep the same card for all the games?"

"Oh, that is because that card gives me luck, I win once in a while."

He didn't want to keep the ongoing conversation because he found out that she was not clear about the possibility of a biased selector. Intelligence, explained Jeremy, is a very general mental capability that, among other things, involves the ability to reason, plan, solve problems, think abstractly, comprehend complex ideas, learn quickly and learn from experience. It is not merely book learning, a narrow academic skill, or test-taking smarts. Rather, it reflects a broader and deeper capability for comprehending our surroundings—'catching on,' 'making sense' of things, or 'figuring out' what to do.

Individuals differ from one another in their ability to understand complex ideas, to adapt effectively to the environment, to learn from experience, and so on. Although these individual differences can be substantial, they are never entirely consistent: a given person's intellectual performance will vary on different occasions, in different domains, and judged by different criteria. The three main processes underlying intelligent thought are encoding of stimuli (how we store knowledge), the inference of relationships (how we reason), and application of relationships (how we make decisions).

It is evident that Bingo players were counting frequent numbers as anyone else. The encoding of stimuli let them store frequent numbers. They inferred relationships between frequency and cards. Players made decisions, selecting a particular card for every game. It was not simple luck, it was a built-in advantage for those players that paid attention.

Newcomers were in a disadvantaged position because they didn't know what numbers were drawn with more frequency. For experienced players, it was a way of benefiting from the knowledge of many bingo nights, building statistics on winning numbers and choosing good cards.

The next night, at 8 o'clock, Jeremy said hello to Palmira and checked who the other players were. Before starting to play, he took some time to choose two cards with the most frequent numbers he recalled. He started to win at least two or three games in a row, and he thought, "OK, now I can start to win some hands, everything is not going to be lost. I am going to recover my money. I'll finally be happy again. You are happier when things go your way."

That night he felt better, "Now I am leveled with the rest of players, we all know how to choose a good card. The system allows us to choose a card and keep using it the next day." He remembers recovering some money; he had a few lucky wins. He didn't think they were rigging anything on purpose to let him win, it was the card chosen that had some of the more frequent numbers. He recovered some lost money, just enough to get comfortable. It was a strange feeling, first, he did not trust the other players, thinking the game was rigged and now he felt so good because of winning a few games, it meant he started to have confidence in the establishment.

At this point in time, Jeremy thought, "I feel good winning, but so good, that I do not want to criticize the organizers anymore." Suddenly, he noticed that he was possessed by gambling, he was not in charge of his feelings anymore. "Why do I agree now with the gaming system? Of course, it is because I am winning, I became another follower of the system, I have become as most people, supporting a bad system because I get a financial gain." He felt scared with the comparison, was he going to support a bad socialist regime now by getting some benefit? The same feeling of winning in the Bingo game applies for socialists, you get benefits and you support the regime. The only ones that can produce a change in the country are those that have not gotten a benefit from the regime, let us start!

A few days later, he started to notice that some frequent players' family members had an excellent night winning streak, their numbers kept coming out on every hand; one player earned 1500 Pesos in about an hour. Jeremy will not forget the face of the player, he was fat and dark skinned, with a strong stare and a small mustache, Jeremy told him, "Why the number 8 is coming out almost every hand and it happens to be that you have most of your cards with the number 8?" the man didn't answer, stared closely at Jeremy, and turned his neck to the other side, Jeremy started to become suspicious of cheating.

The next day, he asked Palmira about the incident, "why the number 8 was being called so often?" He also asked about the guy getting so many winning games. Palmira said that it was normal for somebody to win strike games and make a big profit. However, she said to be careful of not getting in trouble with that guy, because he used to work for the police and had some ties with the government, more precisely the intelligence police. Jeremy said that he was just curious about somebody winning so much and so often. He said, "I hope the guy of the number 8 does not play anymore, he is too lucky."

Afterward, he thought, if I accepted the conditions, I shouldn't be suspicious; we are all allowed to choose our cards. If all choose their cards there is not a dishonesty problem, I shouldn't be complaining. However, a fair play means not choosing your cards for each game; I am going to propose that in the future. Jeremy came back to his suspicious behavior, things were not improving.

Next time, after saying hello to the players, Jeremy tried to fetch the same lucky cards he had before, but he didn't find them. He was not sure if they hide the cards on purpose or some other player had taken them. He had to conform to choose other cards, and he was not so lucky that night. To choose a good card you need good memory and time to choose from the stack of cards; that day he had no patience to fetch a good one.

Because Jeremy knows that any mechanical device can be biased, either because of the selector or because of the balls, he told organizers about the possibility of making some changes on the way the game was laid out. For example, choose the cards randomly, instead of each person keeping the same card over and over. He said, "I noticed that there are some numbers that appear more frequently than others."

Palmira looked him with wide eyes and said, "Yes, I have noticed that myself, but why is that happening? I don't understand."

"I don't know why, maybe some balls are smaller or they are heavier, whatever. Could be that the mechanical selector is biased in some way. Why don't we try to shuffle the playing cards and let players pick them up randomly? I am not suggesting that you change the way you have played all these years, but we can do changes just once, to test how it goes."

Palmira didn't pay much attention to his inquiry. For Palmira, it was important to win sometimes, at least not lose every time. The next days they didn't invite Jeremy, he saw Palmira and her friends playing in hiding. He didn't play anymore either because he went back to the capital the following weeks, but he felt something he said about changing the game was not well appreciated.

The experience with the Bingo game was fruitful; it gave Jeremy some arguments to analyze the relationship of daily experiences with the support to a bad political regime. It was evident that people kept playing because there was some benefit, won games once in a while and not everything was losing. They accepted their participation in a rigged process provided winning a few games. Even Jeremy was feeling good when he started to win a few consecutive games, was thinking on forgetting all his complaints. That is human nature, people are weak, accept rigged situations because there is some benefit around. The political arena was similar people supported a bad regime because they were getting small advantages from their acceptance of injustice.

Those days were the latest he visited the town, didn't come back to play Bingo. Before leaving the town Jeremy was going back to the house one morning, he saw Charlie and said, "Hello there, how are you doing? What are you doing? Are you busy right now?"

"Yes, but come in anyway, I am going to take a break."

Charlie is one of those people that use to arrange the house even if there is nothing to improve; sometimes he opens some holes on purpose to have something to do. Some neighbors say that Charlie's house is evolving badly, that his house doesn't look good, that things are misplaced. Sometimes he builds some walls and puts some doors that make the house look ugly, then he has to bring the walls down and patch the damage.

Jeremy asked him why he didn't go play Bingo at Palmira's house.

"Oh, I used to play Bingo long time ago, but I was losing most of the time. I preferred to abandon."

"Do you think they play a rigged game?"

Charlie understood Jeremy was having some issues regarding the Bingo game and said, "I would say no. But they have played that game for so long that they know what numbers come frequently and what cards are the best ones. They have been using the same selector and the same balls for many years."

"But why some balls come up more frequently than others?"

Charlie simulating a good scientist said, "Any mechanical instrument has some built in tendencies. What happens is that people in town don't care, just want to have a good time. They want to win as much as they can, of course."

SOCIALIST BINGO - Germinal Boloix

Jeremy has a mixed up opinion about Charlie and preferred not to stay long, his lack of imagination is sometimes counterproductive. After the leader of the revolution died, Jeremy recalls asking Charlie why the leader stopped talking for many months before his death, while living in the Island. At the time, nobody knew what was going on, the leader did not speak, people knew the guy had cancer, but Jeremy has known lots of people with cancer that keep talking until they die. The leader was not characterized for being mute, spent hours and hours talking on TV, people used to get bored of too much talking.

During a conversation sitting on the porch with Charlie, other five neighbors and some kids playing around, Jeremy asked, "Why the leader of the revolution stopped talking several months before dying?" Jeremy pointed Charlie out to give his version, but because of his lack of imagination, the only thing he did was to point Jeremy back, "I don't know, you tell me!"

He remembered a picture in the newspaper and said, "I saw a picture of the leader with his daughters when he was sick, and his face was like a dummy, having lost consciousness, becoming a smiling mummy." There were many other possibilities, maybe he was on painkillers and was sleepy, or was unconscious and couldn't talk. The problem was that Charlie was incapable of giving a reason. And this was not the only time Jeremy noticed his lack of imagination, it happened often.

A neighbor suggested, "I believe that the leader was dead long time ago, he couldn't talk because he was dead." The neighbor demonstrated much more imagination compared to Charlie. Jeremy didn't appreciate Charlie's muteness, looking like somebody being attacked by a question, instead of enjoying time and giving imagination a break.

The leader of the revolution, Jeremy found out later according to some news, died of a massive heart attack after great suffering and inaudibly mouthed his desire to live. He couldn't speak because of a bronchial infection. It seems he had several of those infections, had a tracheal tube implanted, his breathing insufficiency persisted and couldn't speak. The information appeared in some newspapers a few months later. According to other sources, remembered Jeremy, doctors in the Island misdiagnosed his cancer, treating him with chemotherapy and other treatments not designed for his cancer. His disease became resistant and impossible to be treated; his quality of life was also affected, as well as his life expectancy. All this explains a bit more why the leader became mute for many months.

The analogy between the Bingo experience in Beach Town and the decisions people make supporting a bad new socialistic regime demonstrates the impact of common activities in the political arena. In the same way, the organizers of the bingo behave, letting persons keep their cards for every game and establishing their own rules, demonstrates some degree of irresponsibility. When they vote during each election, don't analyze the whole picture, do not see the future impact, just see their own temporary benefit, what's in there for me?

In a formal Bingo set up, there are some rules that are suggested to avoid any advantage by some smart players. Usually, players are not allowed to choose their cards, shuffling makes them randomly distributed. The selector and the balls are usually checked out for malfunctioning, completeness or possible rigging. Weighing the balls, checking their sizes and counting how many balls we got should be a common practice. In Beach Town, people were not losing their time on number checkups, just wanted to play the game, but choosing their cards. In the same way, Bingo players at Beach Town keep their cards for all the games, they try to keep their advantages in the society, whatever they are. The country is subject to the same reasoning, don't be fair on common practices, avoid changes in the country, let us keep our own advantages, honest people do not matter.

Comments about Bingo/Society

"In the same way of playing informal Bingo demonstrates how people behave in a society"

"People playing informal Bingo want to keep their advantages, it took them some time to discover, they do not want to lose that marginal benefit and they do not want to listen to critics"

"People who play informal Bingo think they know too much, that they are too smart, they think others are not aware of injustice"

"The rules of informal Bingo are made to benefit the organizers and those that find out what advantages are built into the game"

"The experience playing Bingo shows how weak persons are. If you accept an injustice in the Bingo game because of some benefit, you can accept an injustice in society because you can get a benefit in your life"

Chapter 12: Back to the Future

Jeremy has always considered himself prone to justice and solidarity, independently of politics. But as a good philosopher, he has his doubts about too much government intervention in the life of citizens. He feels democracy has plenty of problems and regarding orthodox socialistic regimes has serious doubts about its viability. That type of regime, being oppressive, restrictive of freedom, choice, and personal autonomy, cannot succeed in the future. One alternative is a balance between capitalism (democracy) and social help; liberty provided in capitalism and social benefits. With all their defects, democracies still provide a practical solution for prosperous societies.

In a sport, the political notion has less influence, the sport objective is not related to politics. However, what can be done is to simulate in the sport, the same political directives utilized in a society. The socialists politics applied to soccer, are going to demonstrate the absurdity of the socialist approach.

The objective of soccer is to get the ball into the other team's goal by using any part of the player's body except his hands and arms. The goalie is the only player allowed to touch the ball with the hands and arms and then only while he is located in his own penalty area.

A referee is in charge of the soccer game. A referee's main objective would be to make players obey the rules and keep the safety of the players. It is the referee's responsibility to ensure that the game remains fun for everyone, players, spectators and officials.

The main rules are related to the field and its dimensions, the ball and its size, the number of eleven players in each team, the officials helping the referee, the duration of the game, the kickoff to start the game, balls in and out of play, the method of scoring, the offside rule, fouls and misconduct, free kicks direct or indirect, penalty kick, throw-in and goal kick, and corner kick. Some additional considerations relate to strategies of attack and defense, how to act appropriately and respond to any situation.

As one of America's most famous soccer fans, former Secretary of State Henry Kissinger, once wrote: It's no accident "that no team from a communist country (except Hungary, in 1954) has ever reached the World Cup finals or semifinals. Too much-stereotyped planning destroys the creativity indispensable for effective soccer."

A few weeks later, Jeremy met his friend Joseph. He knows him from secondary school, they used to study together for the exams and they went together to Sunday afternoon movies. He recalled those happy days, the friends at school, the girls, the teachers, the experiences and conversations they had. It was a travel 'Back to the Future' for him, an agreeable one. Jeremy called Joseph and invited him to a coffee shop close to the apartment. It has been several years since they met. The usual worries are, how are my friends getting old? How do they look? Do I still recognize them? Jeremy was waiting at a table when Joseph arrived. He is tall and has always worn glasses. His glasses look like the bottom of a beer bottle. After saying hello, the initial conversation started by asking whether they had seen old high school friends.

Joseph was happy to talk about those days and said, "I have not seen them lately, I saw two of them just after my graduation from the University."

"I have seen one of our peers, the one that was quite skinny and lived near the school."

His friend was transported mentally back on time and said, "Yes, of course, I remember him, I went at least once on his car, it was a Pontiac Belvedere, convertible, automatic transmission, hydraulic steering wheel, and so on, a very nice car."

"I still remember one of our fellow female friends, the one that was so beautiful and I couldn't ever get a date with her. Remember, the one with green eyes. I have not seen her anymore. How is she now, fat like a sponge?" asked Jeremy joking.

Joseph, knowing more details about her life, said, "Yes, I remember her, she was really beautiful. You know that the skinny guy with the nice car took her for a ride and had a few kisses with her."

"Don't tell me that, I didn't have a nice car at the time, no car at all, the girls didn't smile much at me because I had no car, I suppose."

His friend with unexpected philosophical knowledge said, "Life is like that, females have a built in instinct related to economic and pleasure interests. Males, on the other hand, are inclined to pleasure only."

The conversation continued, remembering some events, such as getting punished for defending one of our mates; the one that put all the chairs upside down in the laboratory and the teacher wanted to expel him from school. Because nobody had seen him, the teacher asked who did it, she suspected it was him. He was the son of a government minister that was already expelled from other schools. Male students decided, as a

SOCIALIST BINGO - Germinal Boloix

group, to confess all were involved in the event to avoid his expulsion. All, except one, got suspended for a week; this guy was the first on the list, and when the teacher asked, he panicked. Jeremy remembers his mother explaining our solidarity position during a special meeting at the school. The teachers' meeting voted against us, independently of the reasoning behind it.

Jeremy started to explain his plans of comparing games and society and the political strategies related to capitalism and socialism. He also said that he was inclined to some type of democratic capitalism with social considerations.

"Great Jeremy, by the way, have you been watching the Euro Champions or the American Coup?"

"Of course, did you see the penalties last night? Chile beat Argentina in the final, Messi was unhappy for sure."

Joseph was very interested in soccer and said, "Today I want to watch the UEFA Champions League game: Spain, Italy. It is starting soon."

"OK, but before you go watch the match, let me explain my approach to demonstrate the difficulties of socialism, using an analogy with Soccer. Let us say that a society is represented as a soccer game, there are two teams and they know that to win means to get some goals. The players know that to win they need to collaborate, as well as to give their strongest effort. The approach to win may be capitalist or socialist."

"Listen, Jeremy, a society is totally different than a Soccer game, how do you dare to make such a comparison?"

"I understand, other friends have told me the same, but I want to show that socialist policies are dangerous in soccer as well as in a Society."

"OK, I see, well, you are the one documenting the results. I am sure you will place things in context."

"It is just a way of comparing two political approaches to a society using a known sport. Capitalists go direct to the point, to win the game. Socialist use to apply strategies that are not well thought and deviate from the objective of winning the game."

"Socialist countries use to participate in the World Cup and they do OK, independently of politics. Socialists have never won a Cup, you know?" said Joseph.

"OK, I see your point, I know Socialists are not made to win, but let me present more details first."

"You know, I am a soccer fan, I use to watch the European and World championships. I know a lot about how the teams are managed, how the teams stay or leave a certain league, who the owners are, who are the players, how much the players get paid, and so on. However, I do not know much about politics" said Joseph, demonstrating he spent all these years working only.

"Listen, Joseph, I don't know so much about leagues and tournaments and owners or players. I am suggesting the analogy for purposes of understanding the influence of a capitalistic or socialistic point of view in the society, using sports."

"The scope of your idea can make a difference; it would be easy to make an analysis of any two teams playing under certain rules, independently of country, league and general management."

"That is right, but because games are played in a certain context, the organization of the players is important for the objectives," said Jeremy.

Joseph listening to the rest of explanations about soccer seemed tired and said, "Let us ask for a coffee first, while I think about all this. By the way, is it possible to smoke in here?"

"Don't tell me that you smoke. I never started smoking, I found it so distasteful."

His friend put his mind on the past thinking about his parents and said, "Remember, in my home, my father was a heavy smoker, and it was my mom who died first from lung cancer. She did not smoke."

"Yes, I remember one of your brothers telling me what happened."

"It is very difficult to get rid of this vice I need to smoke every day."

"You know what my advice is: quit smoking! I know you are not going to follow my suggestion anyway."

After drinking the coffee, they spent about an hour talking about the approach. At the end, Jeremy said goodbye to Joseph and promised to send him a copy of his studies about games and politics.

Two or three weeks later Jeremy went back to Beach Town. As usual, he followed the same routine of getting up early, taking the subway, then the bus and arriving at the town. During the trip, Jeremy wondered, "Why I don't like routine jobs but I love my daily activities of reading and writing?" Jeremy loved research, spent long hours reading and making notes on important subjects and proposing new approaches. He disliked routine jobs at the office, such as supervising other people instead of doing the job himself, he didn't like to take care of other's job.

He worked in research and teaching at the University for many years. Researching was his best experience, it involved creativity, which he loved, but was a solitary activity. Teaching, on the other hand, was amusing, it was normally not creative at all but he felt relax after a class. In class, he watched the faces of the students, some were interested in the subject others weren't. Some students were excellent, for Jeremy, those were the students that used to participate in class, asked questions and challenged the material and the professor. While thinking about his experiences and some of the boring tasks he had to do during his life, his mind came right back to the subject that interested him the most, sports and socialism.

There is a friend of Jeremy that lives 150 kilometers from Beach Town, his name is Gaudi. They worked together at the same oil company several years ago. At the time, the country took control of the petroleum operations, nationalizing production and export. Gaudi is from a neighboring country, the Brother Republic, but has lived for many years in Small Venice. Jeremy believes his friend is a very intelligent man, astonishingly educated and well mannered. He was in charge of the Petroleum Technical Information Support Department, where Jeremy was a software engineer.

Gaudi had already many years of experience in computer science and petroleum operations. The Department had about 20 other analysts and programmers, servicing the geology and operational oil production. Jeremy remembers many peers and the work being done. He was in charge of supervising a group of five analysts for the maintenance of software development projects. One important project involved the establishment of a huge database for the industry, they had to meet with the Ministry of Oil Resources several times and produce file structures and databases. He remembers Gaudi helping during the documentation of the information systems. There were at least 500 different files, several of them having relationships with each other.

Several years later, when Jeremy went for postgraduate studies, he visited Gaudi to gather some data for his research on Evaluation of Software System. He provided several examples of systems to be evaluated and Jeremy was able to produce a paper with his findings. He always thanked Gaudi for his contribution and had him in high esteem.

Today, Jeremy planned to present Gaudi his ideas comparing soccer and politics. He would start by making a list of important subjects to define the framework: rules, players, referees, fans, as well as socialism and capitalism characteristics. The issue of fans participation was unclear, Should fans have a say on the framework? He called Gaudi and they decided to meet at his farm the next day. The farm is half an hour from Spirited Port, the biggest city close to Beach Town.

Gaudi has had divorce problems lately. It seems his hobby was to travel to the farm every week and his wife didn't appreciate his absence. The couple didn't agree on traveling together to the farm and day by day became unfriendly. The conclusion was a divorce. Gaudi had to offer his house at the capital and conform to keep some cash and the farm. Gaudi didn't seem very happy with the deal but it allowed him to move on. He is planning to sell the farm and move to Europe with his family, he still has his mom alive. He better hurry up, suggested Jeremy, to stay some time with her mother, life is short. Jeremy lost his mother relatively young and he misses her all the time.

Going to Spirited Port the next morning, Jeremy took a 'carrito,' it takes over an hour to get there using these 'private' cars. Afterward, you have to take another bus that drops you in Chagual, the town close to Gaudi's farm. From there you have to walk 2 kilometers and you find the farm, with lots of trees and shadows. He was lucky that Gaudi sent him a motorcycle to pick him up. The area was known many years ago to hold guerrilla fighters, hidden in the nearby mountains. The farm has a house, asbestos roof, and three rooms. Gaudi was building a new bathroom these days.

There is an annex where Bison, the man in charge of the farm, lives. Bison has a big family with his wife and about eight children. His main income comes from a salary for taking care of the farm and the crops, besides, Gaudi asks him for extra help cutting weeds and growing trees. Bison gets additional revenue by doing these tasks; many members of his family get extra rewards helping him. In a farm with no income, there is no major source of profit; Bison is the only one getting a benefit. He earns a living, feeds his family, and Gaudi is paying for it. Guess what? I am sure that Bison wants a piece of the pie because this is the way workers feel: "I have been working all my life here and the owner is the only one going to get benefits for the farm? I want at least half of the farm."

This is the way more workers and poor people see the social problem. They believe that justice means it does not matter how you bought your property, what sacrifices you made, how many years of savings it took to purchase; it does not matter if the property gives any benefit or not, workers believe they deserve a percentage of it because they work there. If a property produces a fair amount of income, it is possible to share earnings with your workers, but with no earnings at all, there is no way. Worst of all, some properties lose value over years independently of inflation, the price in dollars is always below the initial price and owners are not able to recover their investments.

"Good morning Gaudi, How are you?"

"I am very good, I just finished my chores this morning. I cut lots of weeds around the plantation, now we have lots of time to talk. Do you know that I have been thinking about what you suggested about sports and politics?"

"That's fine, Gaudi, let us talk about your ideas and the scope of the study, remember that I am doing something nobody has done before." Jeremy presented all his findings during the next half an hour.

"First of all, tell me how socialism and capitalism relate to the analogy. What principles are the players going to follow that differentiate a socialistic approach from a capitalistic one?" Said Gaudi, demonstrating how deep he thinks.

After a couple of hours talking and walking around the farm, Gaudi invited Jeremy to have lunch in town. They sat at a local restaurant and asked for some BBQ chicken with cassava. During lunch, they still had some more chances to talk about soccer and politics. Gaudi identified several points important for the approach. After lunch, Jeremy decided to go back to Beach Town because public transportation is not very reliable late in the afternoon.

The hours had elapsed and Jeremy had to start moving to return to town. He said, "Gaudi, please stay in touch with me, use any communication method you find available. Let me know if you finally move to Spain or not." He promised Gaudi to show his results about the study and left on foot to the nearest bus stop.

"Sure I'll do, nice to meet you again. I love what you are doing, it keeps you busy" said Gaudi.

Back in the capital a few days later, Jeremy found his neighbor Prescot; he lives in the same building and is a soccer fan. Jeremy told him, "Let us go for a coffee, I may have an interesting conversation with you." Jeremy started to explain all his research on the matter of soccer and socialism.

After some time of reflection, tasting his coffee, Prescot asked, "Are one team socialist and the other capitalist? Or is it possible to have both socialist or capitalist teams?"

"Let us review these alternatives: 2 capitalistic teams, or 2 socialistic teams, or one capitalistic and one socialistic."

Prescot started shaking his head, "This may get complicated, there are three alternatives; do you think we have time to analyze all of them?"

"Let us try!"

"Jeremy, I better will meet you later, I have to do some work right now, see you in the afternoon."

Prescot has been living in the same building for over 40 years, his parents bought the apartment and he inherited. He knows everything going on in the building, types of problems, kind of people living in, troubles happening over the years, and so on. Prescot is a very humanist person, always tries to help in the building and has been always related to the condominium decisions; he used to belong to the condominium directive, but because of other's people wrongdoings decided to quit. After his mother and father died, he decided to move to another city because of problems with his brother. Later on, he decided to move back into the apartment, doing some bakery type of jobs, but because of food scarcity he had to do whatever he found available, the economic situation was bad for everybody.

Prescot was explaining the actual situation of water rationing, how people suffered every day waiting for its arrival. Those in charge of opening the faucets had different criteria, some of them were rational, they knew when water was entering the building and were more flexible with the time. But there was an old lady that was totally inflexible when she was in charge of opening the faucets, she applied just one rule, half an hour exactly, she did not take in consideration if water was entering the building or not; more than once Prescot was soaked during his shower, he had no time to rinse, the lady had turned off the faucets. This is a simple example of society mismanagement, people have no brain and apply simple rules to avoid mistakes.

That afternoon, the ring sound and there it was Prescot again, ready to discuss the impact of a particular political strategy in soccer. They went back to the coffee shop and Jeremy started talking about capitalism and socialism. Capitalism can be defined as a structure where there are free market and open competition among participants, some succeed while others fail. In a true capitalist system, success is rewarded and failure is penalized. Socialism, on the other hand, has mechanisms that address unequal situations and prosperous participants find themselves leveled down. A capitalist approach should recognize that sports are a business as any other activity. It also recognizes that a competitive balance among teams provides more interested fanatics, producing at the end bigger revenues. Talking about revenues in a socialist approach makes no sense, but that is precisely a characteristic of socialism, absurdity.

His neighbor was not aware of political approaches and looked confused, "All this is Chinese to me, I am not used to all these political concepts. But I understand collectivity and individuality related to politics."

"OK, then let us better stay close to the sport: rules, players, technical directors, referees, and strategy and I take care of the relationship with politics."

They spent a couple or hours talking about Soccer and Society, at the end, Jeremy got a better understanding of his approach.

About Soccer and Socialism/Capitalism

"Everybody knows more or less the rules of the game, it's the interpretation of the rules and the decisions referees and players make, that have an impact on results"

"Referees are the little bureaucrats on the field, some kind of lawyers or judges, the ones that may have a big influence on the results of a game"

"Capitalists impulse players' merit, therefore, more quality players on the field"

"Capitalists are motivated by winning and fame, a human value"

"Socialists ideas of solidarity and loyalty are against triumph"

"Socialist use to impose incapable players in the field, only because of their loyal to socialism, therefore fewer chances of winning"

"Socialist play minimal effort, just to comply with the Politburo, therefore, fewer chances to win"

"Socialists are going to follow very precise patterns. Players get amused passing the ball around, as players from the Brother Republic did in the eighties with the famous curly hair player, without goal production. It wouldn't be important to have the best players on the field, only fanatics, loyal to socialism, are going to be kept in the lineup."

"Socialists are motivated by control; punishment is applied after the game to those players that don't obey authoritarian orders"

"Socialists select players that think collectively, players that are loyal to the socialist party. Players must be submissive and collaborative, never individualistic. Socialistic players must obey the leaders without complaining."

"Socialists plan the game in excess, expecting players to follow the plan at all cost"

"Capitalists plan the game, but adapt to the opponent, therefore are more flexible"

"Capitalists play both styles: individual and collective, to get goals. They would be more productive for their flexibility, therefore more goals are possible."

"It is important to consider preparation for the games, as well as the strategies during a game. Socialists and capitalist must be doing their effort to compete"

"Socialist play the collective game, pass the ball to get amused, winning is not important"

Chapter 13: In Defense of the Lost Revolution

The new socialist regime of Small Venice calls itself Twenty-First Century Socialism. This Socialist regime has ruined the country in the same way others socialist movements have done in the world. Absurd Socialism took aim at private enterprises in an extermination kind of war, most companies going bankrupt. The government controls all the Institutions: Executive, Military, Judiciary, Electorate, Health Care, Education, Communications, Transportation, Construction, Imports and Exports, Petroleum, Banks, Exchange Rate. Everything has to go through the government's bureaucracy, only the National Assembly is still free. Today there is no food, medicines or services, people has to ask for food in long lines, going through harsh times, dying of hunger every day, and waiting for medicines and medical services. Let us add to all this crime and delinquency rooted for so many years in the country.

The socialist government of Small Venice is a rigged case of Parliamentary Socialism. It was a fraudulent and shameless way of imposing socialism, disguised beneath a Democratic Constitution. According to them, it is inevitable that the working class would become an electoral majority in a democracy, vote for socialism, and the leadership will impose their unjustified desire to limit freedom. It is the ancient Marxist dream, inevitability is built into their genes there is no alternative, according to them. The People must obey the Marxist law. "In your dreams!" thought Jeremy.

The leader of the revolution got the support of the military and crushed any opposition demand to obey the Constitution. The main objective was to control all the Institutions with militants of the party in power. Military personnel got management jobs in the government and collected double salaries, one in the military the other in the government administration. Public Institutions punished defectors by cutting their wages or laying them off. There are millions of people affected by the Discriminating List, used to identify defectors of the regime. Absurd Socialism is another example of failed socialism, and worsened its performance by applying sectarian discrimination.

Common people don't care very much about the name of the system: democracy, socialism, communism, anarchism or capitalism. They are interested only in paying their bills, getting basic supplies, helping their kids during their early years, and being able to enjoy life, at least a bit.

Most people couldn't differentiate a democracy from a dictatorship. Whether the Institutions were kidnapped or not by the Executive was not their problem, they were busy earning a salary. Why should they bother for libertarian ideals?

It is necessary to understand human nature, where complexity prevails, and many different points of view are available. Jeremy cannot stand somebody blindly supporting the regime, he prefers people with criteria. What goes inside the mind of those people obeying blindly? Is there some idiosyncratic aspect he does not understand? Luckily for him, there are some families around that used to support the regime before and now are against it.

It has been the fault of the socialist administrators not building a prosperous country. Corruption has been always blamed for its underdevelopment, but it is just one factor among many others, there are unavoidable cultural reasons. Some do not take the time to learn others do not care or love to take it easy. For many years of dictatorships and democracy, the country didn't improve as expected, but socialist additionally divided the country and mismanaged the resources worse than others. Once the socialist got power, they established a Proletariat Dictatorship using the legal system on its behalf and controlling all the Institutions. It was worse than Nazis in Germany.

There is a scarcity of basic foods and supplies, medicines, hospital services, transportation, education and social well-being. Today, the minimum wage is not enough to survive, a single person requires at least three minimum wages to buy food monthly. At the exchange rate of the black market, a minimum wage is equivalent to 15 American dollars. It is possible to state that the problems in the country could increase because of the idiosyncrasy of people. If people stay submissive, there is no chance for a change. Idiosyncrasy defines the peculiarity of people; a person's own attitude, how do people feel, react, behave and so on. To make things worse, the last government promised exaggerated participation and at the end people did not participate nor improve.

Small Venice was relatively poor before oil was discovered. It was a successful agricultural producer before becoming an oil exporter. Between the years 1920 to 1950, the country started to transform into one of the richest countries in the world. We all know what happen to people that become easily rich: don't do much effort, get consumed by their own richness, become lazy, don't care much. Somebody winning a high prize in the lottery usually gets poor fairly fast, and after a few years starts begging in the streets. Somebody inheriting a fortune gets broke in a few months or years. Small Venice follows a similar pattern, instead of keeping richness to improve prosperity the government has been creating more and more poor people.

According to socialist propaganda, socialism is the government of The People, by The People and for The People. All production mechanisms are in the hands of the government. The State controls and decides on all the instances, but life quality is not among its objectives. Jeremy knew pretty well, everybody going through government controls: education, medical services, transportation, food production and distribution, imports and exports, financial markets, investment opportunities, money exchange rates, and so on.

The Absurd Socialist regime of Small Venice has been in power for 18 years manipulating justice and democracy. All the Institutions are at the service of the leader, there is no independence of powers; orders from the leader are obeyed by all the Institutions. Even with all that control, the government was incapable of handling the country, they thought it was possible to crash the productive culture without damages; they will pay for those mistakes too.

There are still some in favor of the regime; it is their fault to maintain the country stagnantly, helping bureaucrats to ruin the country. Why are all these people still favoring the regime knowing that it is a bad one? Jeremy has been quite curious about that, he wants to find some answers.

When democracy was crumbling and the Absurd Socialism started to take over, the leader of the revolution appeared every day on TV. After a couple of times listening to him, Jeremy remembers having said to a friend, "It is incredible that this guy was elected, you elect somebody that is superior intellectually than you." There are many reasons why some people sympathized with him. Some because of his abundant race mix, the more abundant in the country: white, native and black. Others because he was charismatic, that talked in plain words in your face. Others because he was against Imperialism: boasting about his military strength. Others because he was just like them: coming from the poor. Jeremy thought the guy had some psychological difficulties, probably needing a psychiatrist. The leader couldn't stand a beautiful face in another body; he used to insult petroleum professionals and other careers and dismiss their contribution. It was an insane way of treating people, he was the best the rest were ignorant.

"Anyway, it has to be understood that most people in the country are just too smart, they just follow the flow. They are quite intelligent, making business and profits following the leader so that even their descendants would become rich: politicians, entrepreneurs, and workers benefited from the newly established regime" a friend told Jeremy. "Many politicians, entrepreneurs and intellectuals, calling themselves opposition, profited from the system, making huge benefits."

"The worst of all are those that place themselves in the middle of pro and against the regime, called the "nei-nor" neither in one side nor in the other; they demonstrate not caring about what is going on. At the end, they just want some benefit, walk like zombies within the destruction." Said Jeremy, disagreeing with this type of middle positions; you are in favor or against socialism, there is no middle ground.

Using statistics to determine why some are still supporting the regime is not worthwhile there are as many explanations as individuals. Each person has an opinion about the country, in most cases is personal or subjective, without considering other people's problems. Humans tend to favor things without rationality, just keeping their stubborn position independently of the harm they are imposing on their fellow citizens. Asking for change always starts in a certain point in time; when people cannot stand the regime they do anything to replace it. "If change if for the good, why not?" asked Jeremy, "The problem is if we are wrong in our choice."

Another friend commented a while ago, "It is true, most individuals think different, they don't agree in many matters, that is a characteristic of democracy. Never approve a change towards a new political system that goes against your culture."

Culture is very important, Jeremy agreed, it is not a good idea to test unproven policies in a society. He continued saying, "democracy is not perfect, but it follows our culture; socialists keep doing damage trying to change our idiosyncrasy towards totalitarianism. It is difficult to get rid of a bad socialistic government such as Absurd Socialism because they manipulate those in need."

"If you want to change the government, there is going to be opposition from the minority in power. That happens in Small Venice, the regime stays against the will of the people. They prefer war instead of relinquishing power" said his friend. "Do you remember Hitler's Germany?"

Jeremy had had many conversations with people that provide reasons for supporting a bad regime; they say that the opposition is worse, or want to give more time to the government to do something and so on. Jeremy has his own opinion about a society and the convenience of a capitalistic approach. Only by saying that socialism controls all the means of production is enough of a reason to retire your support. The Absurd Socialism that controls life in Small Venice has had a severe impact on the life of Jeremy and his friends. What was initially a successful career, plenty of opportunities, became a blood, sweat, and tears, kind of experience.

One of his first experiences with a defender of the revolution was a conversation with a neighboring Beach Town man, a few years ago. It happened while drinking a coffee at a local bakery and sharing a table. At the time, April 12, there were many protests involving a jail sentence to a famous political opponent. Scarcity was growing in the country long lines were required to obtain food and basic products at regulated prices.

The man said, "You see, it is the fault of the enterprises, they are not producing goods and services, they want to promote chaos and hunger."

The man didn't see the fault was governmental; enterprises were not able to produce goods and services because of government's cuts on imports by limiting access to dollars. The government was not paying the expenses of imports for months or even years. Besides, enterprises cannot produce at so low prices that don't let them cash some profit. The government had a harsh control on selling prices either.

The man with his small eyes replied, "These enterprises want to get dollars from the government instead of bringing their own pockets' dollars. Why don't they buy the imported goods with their own dollars, instead of asking a favor to the government?"

"In an open society, enterprises buy dollars to import some goods, they make their products, they sell them and make a profit in local currency. In some point in time, they are going to repeat the cycle using local currency to buy dollars. Enterprises are not making a dollar benefit, dollars get spent in each cycle" said Jeremy, using his teacher's speech. One simple example is a bakery, they need some wheat flour to make bread, the country does not produce wheat, therefore it has to come from around the world. They need to buy dollars to import wheat.

The man did not give up and continued, "But why the enterprises don't use their own dollars?"

"Local enterprises are not made to produce dollar benefits, however, global companies do. Global companies bring dollars or goods to the country and expect to make free money exchanges when needed. The government must guaranty the free exchange of currencies." Said Jeremy remembering the problem with the airlines that did not get their money back for their services; they had to stop flights.

The argument could have been going on and on without any error recognition by the man. It is the eternal no budging position; government supporters have a fixed position that never changes, and they believe they are always right. Jeremy found out a few years later the man was a governmental party leader, those defending the government independently of how bad it is. The man, already an old man, uses to wear a T-Shirt with the name of the government party; how can he feel proud? Isn't he ashamed of the worst government in human history? Jeremy knew that many of those supporters were benefiting in one way or another from the government, they had an economic interest in the continuation of the government, it was not precisely because of ideals.

There are of course a few other supporters of the government that don't get any economic benefit, they do it because they interpret wrongly the social-economic situation or they are Marxists that believe that capitalism is a sin. Most of them live above average and have savings or a productive activity allowing them a comfortable life. They don't care about the hardships of other people. However, the reality is that everybody is suffering from the scarcity of food and medicines, as well as high prices; everybody is paying with our limited quality of life.

Another anecdote Jeremy remembers involves a university student. The student was a sympathetic one, those that don't get in trouble in class, independently of critiquing behind scenes. The student was an average student trying to demonstrate that he was making an effort. He always agreed with the professor's comments in class and he tried to find ways of solving any difficult situation among classmates. The student was married and worked in a pizzeria. He used to travel, almost every year, to neighboring countries, to benefit from the government policy of selling cheap dollars for traveling purposes.

One day, Jeremy and the student were walking towards the subway. The student was narrating his experiences in a recent trip, bought an expensive watch and some perfumes, probably to resell them. The conversation started to twist politically, and the student said that during the years of the leader of the revolution things were good, he could provide for his family and had the chance to travel alone once a year. Jeremy told him if you feel that way try to keep benefiting from the government as much as you can because in the future things can change for the worst. The student knew Jeremy was against the government, he looked unconvinced about his advice. Jeremy has not seen the student

SOCIALIST BINGO - Germinal Boloix

since, but knows the student is going to recall his advice: bonanza was not going to stay forever.

Jeremy wanted to talk now with other persons in Beach Town. Minerva, the lady who lives close to the house has a sister, Marylu that is very much motivated to discuss political issues. She has been an opponent of the Absurd Socialism regime since the beginning. She is always reading the newspapers, listening to the radio, keeping in touch with people in Beach Town, and always manifesting her disagreement with the regime. She walks in front of Jeremy's house going to the fish market, where she works. When she walks back to her house, Jeremy is usually in his hammock, reading.

Jeremy has had a few conversations with her about politics and remembers one question, why a bad regime has been in power for so long? Absurd Socialism's government speakers use to say, "We are not yet in a socialistic regime, even though we are trying to build it."

Marylu had an immediate reaction complaining, "Imagine, after 18 years in power, they are still looking for the magical formula. People in Small Venice are suffering the rigors of the scarcity of food, medicines, supplies, services and so on, and the representatives of the government are still talking about building a socialistic society."

"Don't they recognize their failure? Don't they see there is nothing useful in what they have done?" said Jeremy comfortably.

She demonstrated her anger and replied, "Some of these people are there just to stay in power, independently of the results they get. They don't worry about what the people are suffering, they only think about power and their benefit."

"It is a pity that it has been going on for so many years and some people are still supporting the government blindly."

Marylu seemed possessed, her eyes throwing sparks and added, "There has been so much money stolen that they don't want to get punished, they prefer to die before being caught and get sentenced."

She could not stop showed her discomfort and continued, "The Absurd Socialism regime built up a huge political apparatus controlling all the Institutions. Everything is managed by people close to the regime; there is no independence of powers."

She felt like fish in the water and kept going, "I believe besides being a bad regime, they made a huge mistake by controlling the money exchange to a point of paralyzing the economy."

Jeremy knew all about money exchange and added, "The leader of the revolution felt that liberating the dollar price would mean the collapse of his regime, everybody would buy dollars and the country would run out of money for international transactions."

She looked like a financial advisor and said, "If controls had been around only for a few years, to wait for economic stability, nothing would have happened, but it has been going on for more than eighteen years now."

"Of course, it became a discretionary government assignment of dollars to the industry, benefiting primarily supporters of the regime that became phantom entrepreneurs." They used different exchange rates according to services, such as food and medicines, travelers, equipment, and supplies; still others for non-basic imports, such as cars or appliances. They created an exchange differential that was exploited by unconscionable merchants and those supporting the regime becoming rich. Normal people could only buy dollars in the black market.

She added, "Many bureaucrats of the government became rich, making business getting cheap dollars and selling them in the black market. People are not stupid, they see the opportunity and they take it right away."

"That situation is typical of super controlling governments. I believe the severe crisis in the country has a big component on the way the government manages the exchange rate market. Enterprises have been strangulated, without dollars, to the point of bankruptcy."

Jeremy asked, "How do you think is the distribution of support to Absurd Socialism in the community of Beach Town?"

"Some people still support the regime; most of them do it because they get some kind of benefit. Sometimes they get loans, subsidies and other times political influence in the community, some get part-time jobs, and so on. However, lots of people are not getting benefits, and most of them disagree with the regime" said she.

He was thinking in terms of probability and statistics, and said, "Then it is the usual normal distribution, 25% in favor, 25% against and approximately 50% that are not in favor or against."

Marylu, that did not know much about statistics, neither understood where the normal percentages came from, said, "Those percentages have changed dramatically during the last three years of the new President. The distribution is now over 70% against the regime, less than 15% is still in favor and the rest has no strong opinion."

SOCIALIST BINGO - Germinal Boloix

She knew very well the huge amounts of income the country collected and added, "Good luck through huge oil income was transformed into bad luck, people thought that the mirage would last indefinitely, however, the oil prices plunged to historical minimums and the country is bankrupted."

"If socialism was good for the people, and being experienced in a rich country, it would have been a historical opportunity to improve the country and to promote socialism all around the globe. Therefore, this failure is a clear demonstration that socialism is not a solution, is a sin instead."

He wanted to find out what happened in the town and asked, "Marylu, tell me about Beach Town, why some people still support the regime?"

"There are not many work offers; there are few sources of income. As you know, only commerce and construction have some potential market, the rest is government services' offices" said she.

He recalled some neighbors being offered part-time jobs and said, "That is why the municipality engages some workers on administration or providing community services such as kindergarten, financed by the government."

"Notice something, most people that supported the leader of the revolution are not supporting the President anymore, they feel he is not capable of running the country, therefore there is a sentiment against him going around," she meant, independently of how many jobs are offered by the regime, he does not get more support.

He knew about the difficulties fishermen had in town and asked, "What do you think about loans given to fishermen?"

"You know that my family runs a fish enterprise, we have been on it for many years, my father used to be a fisherman himself until he died. There are new fishermen around they took over most of the fishing in town. However, I consider many of them pretty lazy, they are not fishing to provide food for the Town, are fishing just to be able to stay alive, don't strive to produce."

He did notice that there was not much fish in town and said, "Do you mean they got new boats and engines to do nothing? Those boats are financed by the regime, do they pay for their loans?"

"The town is not benefiting from their fishing, they got all that gear for private use, selling only to survive, our money has been lost."

Worst of all, thought Jeremy, is loosing the money and said, "If payments are not collected here in the town, in the case of those fishermen, what do you expect is happening all around the country with so much money invested in unpaid loans?"

Marylu agreed on most of what was said and continued, "In the town, most people are lazy, lack constancy, are not able to work full-time; by the way, it has been like that for centuries. I would say that it is not only socialism fault, it is because people are unproductive."

"Some say that every country gets the government they deserve; it means that we deserve this new socialist regime that doesn't improve the life of citizens" sadly concluded Jeremy.

The regime was bad, Jeremy knew, but he never thought things could go so awful. Jeremy is disappointed in intellectuals that have not provided a comprehensive understanding of the problems of socialism. Intellectuals must take the lead and demonstrate scientifically how bad socialism is. Intellectuals and Philosophers must be the ones in charge of transforming this world for the best. Don't let our civilization on the hands of socialists; masses are blindfolded and capable of self-destruction.

Chapter 14: Difficult Times for the Regime

Complaining wherever you went was popular: at work, with neighbors, at school, on the street, in the metro, in supermarkets, everywhere. Jeremy was startled that so many people didn't say a thing, used to be silent like intoxicated by Scopolamine the drug that limits will. He remembers a small restaurant in downtown, near the Presidential Palace, where he used to drink fruit smoothies. It was the beginning of the regime, he was complaining to the owner about the wrong governmental decisions, while a group of professors was sitting just besides. The owner said that he was doing OK, that everything was going well, his business was booming with the regime. The neighboring professors applauded for his comments, they were pro-regime, at least at that time.

He found the comments disturbing, he felt discouraged, knew he was right, he was an Indigo Child that understood everything, but people around him didn't wake up. Jeremy found out a couple of months later the owner sold the restaurant and embarked to Europe, his homeland. His conclusion was that the owner was afraid of saying the truth against the government and preferred to make his business improve, instead of being honest. He knew he was being observed by partisans of the regime, his location was too close to the Presidential Palace, he was afraid of avengers and not being able to sell his business.

After the years, of course, more and more people were noticing the wrong doings of the regime and started to complain too. Jeremy used to go to street protests and there were many people outside protesting too. Hundreds of thousand participated in hundreds of protests over the years. After the leader of the revolution died, people started complaining louder, we were lucky the revolution died with him. A much bigger protest is needed to get rid of this regime. The last three years have been awful. The scarcity of food and medicines, together with bad hospital services are hurting the people. Life expectancy has diminished, many people are getting sick and dying because of medicine and services scarcity.

Personally, Jeremy was affected because he applied a strict auto-scarcity diet. It was like the case of newspapers auto-censure, quite known those days. Jeremy inflicted on himself a punishment, ate less and followed a strict diet; he did not go on lines to buy regulated goods. Jeremy was not able to get some of the most common foods people used to, for example, corn flour, butter, eggs, mayonnaise, oil, and coffee. He had no access to soap, deodorant, toilet paper, or detergent either. At the beginning, he didn't find eggs but afterward was capable of getting some, paying more expensive prices, of course. He got beef and chicken and vegetables, but prices were always too high, increasing at least 25% per week. His budget was starting to resent the effects of inflation, he started to restrict his expenses on food; he had to buy the minimum amounts of meat, and leaning toward white cheese only. He was able to find ham, buying small amounts. He was directly affected by scarcity of medicines. He needed high-blood pressure and cholesterol medication, had to live without them for a few months; every pharmacy he asked for was depleted.

He started to lose weight fast. His diet was as follow, in the morning, oatmeal with water and powder soy milk, white cheese and cassava. For lunch a piece of fried breaded chicken, boiled vegetables, plantain, and cassava. For dinner, either a piece of breaded chicken with vegetables or white cheese with cassava. He lost more than 15 pounds in a couple of months.

Humans tend to blame others for their problems; Jeremy was human too and blamed the government. The scarcity of food was enough to make him change his lifestyle. In Europe, he was used to very simple breakfasts, cereal, some bread or croissant with butter and coffee. In North America, a common breakfast includes bread and peanut butter and coffee. It is clear that peanut butter contains more proteins than white cheese, he was getting undernourished. In Small Venice, he only found some oats mixed with water and soy milk flour, cassava with white cheese and coffee for breakfast. In Small Venice, the breakfast usually includes 'arepa' with butter, ham and cheese, and coffee, but corn flour was out of reach. Jeremy knew his diet was better than the one Germans gave to Jews, but he was losing quite of bit of weight as concentration camps' Jews anyway.

It is a pity to see people standing in lines very early in the morning, waiting for the trucks arriving at noon. Sometimes the trucks bring some products, other times they don't. The Absurd Socialism approach has been offering low prices, for regulated products, to people that stay on lines, while those that don't, see negated that possibility. Worse of all, now they bring packs of food for those that are in a list; the list includes those identified by the community at the discretion of the party in power. Absurd Socialism is an approach that promotes lists: Old Discriminating List and New Discriminating List. Discrimination has been the most dangerous weapon because it hurts most people.

SOCIALIST BINGO - Germinal Boloix

About ten years ago, Jeremy remembers a Professor asking about the possible reasons citizens had to support Absurd Socialism. Jeremy was sitting at the office and said, "Some people get income from projects financed by the government, others get jobs, full or part-time. The government forces banks to open dossiers to public loans. The government has created a huge bureaucracy with those projects and people did not pay their debts, for example."

The Professor replied, "I do believe the economy has an impact on support, don't forget the high prices of oil, the government is expending lots of money building a network of collaborators using the extra income. People settle for little."

He agreed, "It is a pity that we live in a country where survival only is the rule. Others enjoy only making jokes about the absurdity of the regime but never participate in a protest. They don't care about what others suffer."

However, the economic and health difficulties are creating huge government disapproval. Parliamentary socialism has demonstrated its inefficiency, people prefer to go back to simple capitalistic democracy, where people can live, eat and be healthy. Most people are going through hunger and many are dying of simple diseases.

Maslow's Hierarchy of Needs is a good example of how people behave according to their needs. The first set of needs is Physiological, these are basic: the body craves for food, liquid, sleep, oxygen, sex, freedom of movement, and a moderate temperature. When any of these are in short supply, people feel the distressing tension of hunger, thirst, fatigue and short of breath, sexual frustration, confinement, or discomfort of being too hot or too cold. The rest of needs is organized according to Safety, Love, Esteem, and Self-Actualization. Once a set of needs is satisfied, people can move to the next level.

Fifty years of democracy kept people waving around different levels of needs in a disorganized fashion. democracy didn't solve the problems but kept some people looking for improvements. Absurd Socialism, on the other hand, pushed people below the first level of needs in Maslow hierarchy. Today people live only to satisfy Physiological needs. Ask all these people making lines to buy food whether they are looking for self-actualization. People are looking for basics, time is spent on survival activities, most are in a survival mode, such as did our Neanderthal or Cro-Magnon ancestors.

Lately, the Defense Minister has been appointed to manage food distribution in the whole country; it is clear for everybody that food distribution is not a responsibility of the military, some generals are against populist measures. Radicals want to take absolute power in the country crashing the opposition. The Legislative Power is not welcomed by the President and radicals want to get rid of the Congress. It is unclear whether the military would be involved in a coup they have been enjoying the power and many benefits all these years.

At the beginning of the regime, people felt a sort of economic bonanza, were able to travel, do tourism and buy electronic equipment. However, all these years had unrest, protests, and strikes. It was under the President mandate that the economy crashed and the suffering got manifested in huge lines and monumental scarcity. Food under-supply has been hurting the population these last years. It is a country living in conditions of postwar, preparing for a war.

While Jeremy was wondering about all these issues about a mismanaged country in the hands of a group of radical lefties, a few surprising events started to unfold. Everything started with huge protests at the beginning of Spring 2017 in the capital, the Supreme Court of Justice tried to take charge of the National Assembly through some imprudent and unconstitutional decrees; it was considered as a coup d'etat. People were asking the resignation of the president and changing the government. Several protests built up over the months, causing unrest in the country. A few months later, Autumn brought the news of a military putsch starting in several provinces. People expectations were that things could start to change if a new leadership would take power, getting rid of the regime and finally improve the economic situation. Jeremy expected an end to the socialist regime and a going back to a Social Capitalist Democracy.

A military coup was impossible, the regime spent huge amounts of resources keeping the military under control. However, the news was clear, groups of rebels have taken one of the main forts on the East Side of the country, including the biggest island, Flower Island, at the North-East. Jeremy thought that because a civic-military style of government was in charge, there was not any possibility of changing the government while the military supported the regime.

According to some people, the East of the country was taken by opposition leaders, controlling Flower Island with some international support coming from America and Europe. It is not clear who the names of the leaders are and no news about their whereabouts. What it is known

SOCIALIST BINGO - Germinal Boloix

is that this group of rebels is against the New Orthodox Socialist regime and that they are well armed. It seems a few battleships and an aircraft carrier located around Flower Island, ready to strike in case of need.

At the same time, the West side of the country was taken by armed forces, screaming against the President and in favor of the second in command. It looks like the country has been divided into three or four pieces: one controlled by the government at the Center, and the other two or three controlled by rebels, at the East, West and South. The rebels in the South control the mineral arch that has been recently exploited. The rebel group in the East is attributed to the opposition, but the rest is formed by disbanded sectors of the same political party in power.

The government gave too much power to the military, including the management of oil camps, mineral arch, Central Bank, Imports and Exports, food distribution and infrastructure. The policy of attaching the most delicate matters to the military indicates that their hegemony has been building up. The President is still in power because of the Central Bank and the Gold Reserves, located in the capital. Guess who is suffering all this: The People. Hunger is increasing and there are no policies to solve the problems. It is unclear how the matters are going to be solved, a civil war? a full blown dictatorship? Is the country going to collapse into several pieces?

Radio stations were transmitting classic music and a message from the government saying they fully seized control: the rebel soldiers were going to be crashed and sent to jail. There are at least ten thousand soldiers, around the country, involved in the coup. Jeremy had always thought that the leader of the revolution had in mind the possibility of taking power by brute force anytime. Everybody knows that he came from the military and started a coup several years ago; he was not successful on his initial attempt, but later on won the elections, using his popularity after the coup. The possibility that some of his allies were ready to act using force was always present. What was happening now, who was after the coup?

The President was inviting people to take the streets in a show of support for the government. The whereabouts of the President were not disclosed, he seems to be in a secure location. The President had lately been isolated from the radicals of the political party in power. The main advantage for the President is that he has not been captured and is free and able to use a mobile phone App to call his followers into the streets, where they can dare the troops with war tanks to kill them. Because many of the soldiers located at the Capital hesitate to shoot people, the coup didn't proceed as expected and the country has been divided up to now in four blocks.

He was scared, a military coup going on and he had no food or medicines. Running water was limited because of government restrictions. Electricity was faltering some days of the week. Was he going to make it? Jeremy was in a bad position, was alone in the apartment in the capital and had nobody to call. He had no family around, everybody was struggling for food and medicines nobody was available to help. Neighbors in the same building were not especially nice, thought only about themselves; fetch food and store it into the apartments, nobody opened doors when inquired. One thing Jeremy knew was that dying of starvation usually takes about 6 months; the body takes upon your reserves and keeps you alive; there is always some water and some minimal amounts of food to eat.

The case of sleep deprivation is worst, people can die in a week; the body cannot handle the disorder sleep deprivation produces on the brain. Jeremy thought that if he had survived up to now, it was difficult now to die starved. He had no real problems with sleep anyway, therefore no possibility of sleep deprivation. However, in difficult times, any small illness could be enough to take away a life. There were many examples of people dying in hospitals because of medical, medicine and service difficulties. Some people couldn't get an operation because there were no testing reactors to determine a malady; lots of clinics had no medicines to treat common illnesses.

Protests against the President had grown more and more. His unpopularity is not casual, even though he won the last elections. Jeremy was never convinced of the election fairness, something fishy was going on. It is unclear if the putsch is going to fail or not, many senior army leaders have not been convinced to go along with the government and are disobeying the ruler up to now. The situation may change because hunger and lack of medicines and services are decimating the population; something has to be done right away patience is not a solution. Jeremy wished he knew a high military rank, to make valid his point of view against the government and get rid of the President right away, or at least call a Referendum to reunite the country.

He decided to go outside and find out whether any store was open and buy some food. He got dressed and descended the stairs, the elevator was not working; eight floors down were a pain on his weak knees. Suddenly loud sirens and military trucks passed by. Jeremy went back inside as fast as he could, slammed the doors close. He waited a few instants to see if the soldiers were going to stop nearby. Luckily, the trucks kept on moving and disappeared out of view. Jeremy went back to the streets and started to walk toward the main avenue and noticed all the stores were closed. It was probably too early, still dark in the morning. He didn't know what to do, should he keep walking or go back to the building? Finally, he decided to keep going toward the local Liberator Square. While walking, he thought about the political, economic and hunger situation; they are related, no doubt. His problem was that he was hungry, he didn't care very much about the regime, didn't even care if the government was going to stay or not in power, just wanted to grab something to eat, to make sure he survived just another day.

Whole walking, he was thinking about the social, political and economical situation, hunger and shortages; they were related without any doubt. The problem was that he was hungry, he did not care about the regimen problems, neither whether the government was going to keep power or not, he just wanted to find something to eat, to be sure of surviving just another day. For Jeremy, the situation was worse than what other civilians were going through, he was in the country for short periods of time, he did not store any provisions and he did not like to stay in long lines to buy regulated products.

Malnutrition had affected Jeremy a lot, lost so much weight that felt weak most of the time. His auto-imposed diet, related with scarcity, was making a devastating effect on his endurance. He was unable to think clearly, started to forget simple things too easily. Food and medicines were the only things he kept in memory, forgot about his loved ones, his responsibilities, his friends. He was obsessed with hunger; a piece of 'arepa', a kind of cornbread, with butter was one of his breakfast dreams. He was not able to buy corn flour and had to replace bread for cassava. He remembered how simple his breakfast was in Europe when visiting his family: bread with butter and coffee, and felt full.

In Small Venice, it was not possible to find a simple protein as peanut butter. Lack of proteins is making people weak physically and mentally. Some time ago it was possible to find some raw peanuts at a high price, but lately, it is almost impossible to find them, they were imported from North America. People were depleting stores; one day, he was buying some oats and had a couple of 500 grams packages taken to the till, suddenly dozen of people entered the store and took the rest of packages. The only thing Jeremy was able to find, up to now, for sure was cassava;

people were not so interested in buying it, but things may change in the future.

From the distance, he was able to distinguish some people moving in the same direction, toward Liberator Square. One block or two before arriving, he felt a roar close to his ears, saw a shadow of something moving fast, it was like a rocket, was not able to distinguish it immediately. He stared toward the buildings looking for suspicious stones thrown from the balconies nearby. Suddenly, he saw some black spots, hidden on top of the trees, they were ravens getting together in an aggressive stand. He saw one raven flying low toward people walking by, trying to bite them. The trees were crowded with ravens, he immediately thought about the movie 'The Birds' by Alfred Hitchcock. Jeremy didn't appreciate such birds very much, they were rude and cold, without any empathy whatsoever toward humans. He remembered the Raven by Edgar Allan Poe, one of his best books, a beautiful poem, talking about a raven always unreliable, 'Nevermore'. These birds are capable of devouring a carcass in a few minutes.

Ravens are quite intelligent, can perform tasks in the first trial, compared to other animals that never succeed. Ancient civilizations thought ravens were devilish messengers; when they are around, death becomes the rule. Ravens are scavengers, but they need the help of other animals to open a carcass; they call for help from other animals, by singing and looking for attention. Jeremy thought of a raven biting his eye and emptying his eyeball, it was disgusting. Jeremy was scared, were the ravens hungry because of the scarcity in the country? Could they hit your eyes and make you blind? Could they empty your eyeballs? This were hard times, ravens were the messengers of death and danger, the future was bleak, some things were going to happen in the country, very bad events were approaching. Was Jeremy going to be hurt by those future events?

Ravens live primarily in North America, they are not found in South America. He established the birds were crows instead, a black bird, smaller than ravens and it is not characterized by his intelligence. He felt scared anyway these flying birds look dangerous and were all around on top of the trees in a threatening attitude.

According to the official news, people started to get close to Liberator Squares around the country, to support the government. Jeremy didn't see too much movement close to him, he heard some people talking about the putsch, "It seems the second in command, you know this preposterous guy, the guy that is always insulting every politician, the ex-military

SOCIALIST BINGO - Germinal Boloix

captain, who has been looking after power for many years, is behind the coup, but nobody knows where he is." Because the guy is an ex-military officer, has some empathy from the military; he seems to be quite radical, capable of establishing a cruel regime to crush the opposition.

People at the square didn't look aggressive, even though a few of them were wearing shirts with the name of the government party. Jeremy knew from experience that he had to be cautious, saying things against the government would imply a possible fight. He was not strong enough for a fight, felt dizzy and was hungry; hunger is contagious, watching others increases your desires to appease it. He recalls years before when he was protesting against the leader of the revolution, other people watched him with no empathy. Today, instead of supporting or rejecting the government, people were asking what was going to happen with food supplies now. If there were food problems before the coup, now scarcity would grow much bigger.

Before the leader died, Jeremy screamed, "Long life to the leader, in the Island!" Once dead he said, "He won't come back! He is dead!" He was imitating the pro-government slogan, 'They won't come back,' people's pro-regime used to say against the political opposition. People pro-regime didn't appreciate Jeremy's jokes, were obsessed with the deceased leader. It was an insane love for a leader; according to Jeremy, the leader didn't deserve love at all.

The official news lately reported, "There seems to be an uprising in the military, we are not really sure who are in command. Once we determine who the officers are, we are going to act against these groups. The American Empire is behind this uprising, capitalism wants to crush the revolution they want to take our petroleum. Long live the leader of the revolution." Hours after the coup began hundreds of soldiers have been reportedly killed in the attack. However, two big cities have been occupied by rebels at the East and West of the country. The rebels on the South are distributed in a large area because the mineral camps are widespread.

A loud explosion was heard in the capital, fighter jets buzzed overhead, gunfire erupted outside military headquarters. It is not the first time a coup has damaged the country; years ago, the leader of the revolution was allegedly involved in a putsch and was incarcerated at the time for a few years. Afterward, the disaster of his government, the worst of human history. It seems the rebels wanted to attack the President and had bombed places he had been at shortly after he left. The President evaded death by minutes. Several soldiers, in helicopters, descended on his vacation house near the airport, on ropes, shooting, just after the President had left, in an apparent attempt to seize him.

Around a dozen individuals have been named among the coup plotters, but in Small Venice, it is difficult to distinguish between real foe and political challenges. The President wasted no time in cleaning out his military. Hundreds of officers, soldiers and other suspects, linked to the coup, have been arrested, authorities said recently.

Up to now, the government was controlling the media. If the country is divided, the probability of hunger would increase exponentially. Jeremy was not born to suffer so much his body was not so strong and was lacking important medicines to keep up with his health. Even though he was sitting at the Square, his legs started to tremble, he couldn't stop them, they were on a dance on their own, was not in charge of his body anymore, an external force had taken charge.

It is well known that there are militias and 'Tupamaros' in favor of the government, they may strike anytime. These groups have been armed by the government and have been helping the President to stay in power; it seems hundreds of soldiers and officers have been executed in the streets near the Presidential Palace. Jeremy remembers people dying on the streets because of their opposition to the regime. Bands of criminals used to shoot people in the streets and were never convicted.

He asked about the possibility of having something to eat. One lady told him to wait until 8 am, a store was going to open and he saw people starting to get in line. He decided to move toward the store and got into the line. He asked, "Do you know what they are offering today?" Somebody said, "It seems they are offering some chicken. It is better to get some proteins stocked, in case we don't see them again."

He waited until noon, was starving. A truck arrived and started to unload boxes of chicken. He paid an expensive amount for a kilogram, about one-month minimum wage, but it would assure him a few days of survival. He walked back to the apartment and got some ham and cheese croissant and a coffee in a bakery close by; he ate it right away hidden, to avoid being robbed, and also as in a celebration for being still alive. At the apartment, he prepared some chicken for storage in the freezer and left a couple of legs for today's lunch.

Chapter 15: Aftermath of Harsh Times for The People

After a few days, since the start of the coup, newspapers and television stations, opposing the regime, were closed or new management was brought in. Many journalists and editors have lost their jobs. Users of social media and Internet who criticized the President or the government are landing in jail. The government has been keen to suggest that a small band of low-ranking dissenters were behind the coup, a report and the released names of military figures linked to the plot suggest it ran much deeper. At least 150 of the 360 generals and admirals in the country have been fleeing toward Flower Island, the Independent Republic of the West or the new Mineral Arch in the South. It seems the plot was wider than originally suspected and there are deep divisions within the armed forces. It seems rebels against the regime are invading and taking charge of important cities on the East, West and South of the country.

Definitively, the country is divided into at least four pieces, the President in the Center, supported by the Island and some local armed forces. They are in control of the airport and the main port, allowing them provisions and supplies. They control the main communication resources, including TV, telephone and data transmission. Because of International support, the rebels are still in command of their armed forces in the East. In the West, things are different, the second in command seems to be holding support tight, but there is no news about how are they doing and of his whereabouts. The West is considering separation from the country, an old desire of the population. The West includes the richest provinces, those that produce petroleum, they have been always pushing to separate from the country and become independent. Some non-aligned countries are supporting the West rebels. Zimbabwe, Iran, and North-Korea are among the countries supporting the group.

From the South, news is not clear, it seems greedy individuals are in charge, capable of decimating the opposing population. New named military officers took power and control the Orinoco River and the South Provinces.

Looking at the map, each piece of the country has natural resources to exploit. It seems the party in power had planned that strategy many years ago since the leader of the revolution was in power. It was a strategy suggested by the dictators of the Island to maintain some supremacy in

South America. The three pieces at the North have the Caribbean Sea for transportation and supplies, while the South gets its supplies through the Orinoco River, probably from Guyana.

Civilians started to move towards one of the sides according to their political preferences, a frontier has been built exactly at Beach Town between the Center and the East. Jeremy wanted to go to Beach Town, he had to take care of the house. The problem was that if he did, won't be able to come back to the capital. Additionally, he didn't know what was going on in Beach Town. Was the town taken by rebels or by the government? He didn't know what to do. The other possibility was to go back to North America with his daughters, but there were no flights going out of the country, airports were closed, only military personnel was allowed.

He decided to make a phone call to Beach Town and find out what was going on there. He talked with Marbella and asked her about what possibilities he had, "Here, things are unclear, some days rebels from the opposition are in charge, but others days it is the president's forces."

"Marbella, do you know if it is possible to get there and stay in the house?"

"If you are able to cross the border, you can stay in the house, you have the keys of the house anyway, otherwise you must go back."

He decided to find out whether the buses were working these days. He went with the metro towards the bus station, noticed the station was almost empty, only a few buses going to close destinations. He found out that next weekend buses were going to travel toward the border and they just would get to town and come back, they could not go to the East. He decided to give it a try.

He went next Saturday morning to the station and there was a long line of people already waiting. He was in line already for two hours when about 8 am a bus stopped and people started to get in pushing around. He had to pay whatever the fare was there was no way to argue about prices, take it or leave it. The price was five times more expensive, local currency had lost at least 100 times its value, he decided to go anyway.

The bus stopped several times because the military was inspecting and asking for identification. After a nine hour trip, triple the normal travel time, arrived at Beach Town. It was about 6 pm and he was hungry, got close to the house and passed by Marbella's house.

"Hello Marbella, how are you?" Jeremy said in a hurry.

"Not too good, but alive, things are crazy these days, nobody is able to express its political viewpoint anymore in here. You know that I have always been in favor of the regime, but now I am against. We don't know who is in charge. It is a disadvantage to be on the border between rebels and government."

He could not believe what he heard and said, "Imagine, you have always been pro-government and I am against it. Do you think repercussions against people are possible, because of their beliefs?"

"Of course, something is going to happen, you better be cautious. A war to liberate the country is on its way."

He did not understand quite well what she meant about liberating the country. Was it to liberate from socialists or from rebels? He was hungry and went to buy something to eat, found some cassava and some hot sardines, enough to live one more day. He went back to the house and started to eat desperately, he was more nervous than anything else but did not know why. He took a shower in the evening it was dark already and decided to go back buy some groceries. He found some vegetables and some eggs, together with some cookies; it was enough to have a bite at night and the next morning.

That night he was extremely tired, nine hours in the bus was tiresome. He went to sleep early, around 10 pm, did not want to talk to anybody. After midnight he heard some noises, it was like loud steps, he decided to take a look. He saw military personnel on the street it seemed they were looking for people. He heard a strong noise on the door, banging and shouting. He decided to open, he was not afraid of anybody; he didn't do anything wrong, not even throwing a 'PooTov' bomb to anybody, those bombs full of shit that became famous against government repression. Military personnel told him that they needed to verify his identity. He showed them his ID. The soldier took his ID and went to talk to another officer. After a while, the officer said, "Come with us to the commissary, your name was listed as an opponent."

He arrived at the commissary and a commandant started to ask some questions: "Are you in favor or against the President?"

He knew times were difficult, his thoughts coming and going, "what should I say? I better say nothing because these guys are military and the only thing they know is to obey orders. In fact, he was not in favor of the President but had never done something wrong. After a silence that lasted an eternity, Jeremy answered, "I am not against anybody, I am an intellectual, I want to be a philosopher, I use to write books about the society. I want to live in a better society, I want everybody to prosper."

The commandant seemed to know him pretty well and said, "Listen, according to the information we possess, and we have been observing you over the years, we know that you read a lot of books on your hammock and that you are plotting against the regime. You have been interviewing some people over the years and we know your position against the socialist regime. We know what you think about the government, our information system is updated daily. We don't accept dissidents in our territory. You are not going to criticize the government anymore. Long live the deceased leader of the revolution!"

Jeremy that used to get angry for everything, replied, "I don't agree, I have done nothing bad. Please let me get a lawyer!"

The commandant watched him with a smile and responded, "It seems you don't understand, there is a martial law in effect. We have the right to incarcerate anybody, anytime. You were lucky up to now, moving freely everywhere. You should have been in jail many years ago but the people in the town protected you because you were an intellectual or some kind of thinker or philosopher."

The commandant said that agent No. 8 was the one denounced you, "It seems you were playing some Bingo games and our agent noticed your lack of affinity to our regime and gave your name away to the counterintelligence agency."

"Agent No. 8?" asked Jeremy? "I do not know who that agent might be."

"You will have lots of time in jail to think about who our agent is, do not worry. It is not our fault that you have a gambling problem."

He was sent to a cell with no windows. There were at least 10 people in a small, 3x3 room. There was an odor in the air, like frozen excrement, a type of smell that doesn't explode at your nose, but makes a distinctive effect, easily recognized. Because there was no light, he couldn't recognize other people inside.

A guy started to speak, "It is your turn now, it is a pity you got incarcerated."

He recognized the voice, it was the voice of Charlie, "My eyes are used to the dark, it will take you a couple of hours to get used. I have been in here for a couple of weeks. We should be liberated anytime soon, when the rebels take back the town we will get free."

"Hello Charlie, wow, it is you, I feel relieved, at least somebody I know in here."

He kept chatting with Charlie for a couple of hours. He found out what was going on in town and the country. It seems the coup happened

SOCIALIST BINGO - Germinal Boloix

because the government didn't want to accept the referendum. The international community disagreed with the regime and decided to support some military dissidents that were available for recruitment. Charlie was explaining that the regime was getting support from the Island, and some Caribbean and South American countries, those that received bargaining oil exports during the years of the deceased leader of the revolution.

Jeremy knew most of the news about the coup his doubts were about personal issues and asked, "Why are we in jail without participating in any wrongdoings?"

"It seems the regime got support from the Island's G2 counterintelligence service. It seems they have been following all dissidents and built up a database with information about each one. People we know, on a day to day basis, were in charge of sending information; it was their way to earning an additional income. They know everything we are saying or doing. For example, all your interviews about games and socialism have been tracked down. Even your Bingo games and your complaints to organizers are known by the establishment."

He looked surprised, all his research was known by the government they evidently are against knowledge and asked, "Do you mean they know I am studying and analyzing how bad a socialist regime is?"

"Of course, they are aware of all you do, have ears all around. It seems you said something about bingo and socialism they didn't appreciate at all. Do you know that if they send you to the capital, you may get executed?"

Jeremy, as a good intellectual, thought that ideas should not be persecuted that way, and could just say, "I don't' believe it. It is incredible that such a regime is against knowledge and punish its citizens that way. If socialism doesn't work, better to know it right away, don't dwell in political ideas that are outdated, move to a better approach that takes into consideration idiosyncratic humanity."

"Jeremy, pay attention, the government knows everything about you. They know what books you read while you swing yourself in the hammock. They know what you think, what we all think. It seems in the Island they are experts on telepathic mind readings. A doctor from the Island is capable of knowing what you think even if you don't talk."

He asked Charlie about agent No. 8. Charlie said that he did not know about that. Jeremy told him that while playing Bingo he had some exchange with one of the neighbors because the number 8 was called too often, maybe he was the guy who denounced him. Charlie told him, "That is why it is not a good idea to get involved in gambling, people around are not trustworthy."

Detachment of Retina

A detachment of his retina happened just at the time when the coup was stabilizing and the country was divided into four pieces. There were rumors saying that everything was an invention of the President to stay in power, those changes in the country were happening to keep everything unchanged.

He recalls having the symptoms of a virus and lots of nasal congestion at the time, was a virus, malnutrition, lack of medicines or weakness possible causes of detachment? He was taking some pills for his cold, some he brought for his trip, but they didn't improve his health.

Another prisoner suggested, "Why don't you take some pills we keep here, these are acetaminophen, good for common cold and some others ailments? Let me tell a companion to get a couple of them."

"OK, I will try, I have been with this nasal congestion for a long time and it doesn't go away. I have been taking some pills with acetaminophen too but there is no definitive improvement."

The companion brought him a couple of pills and he took one that night. He noticed that he couldn't sleep well; he felt the pill was not right for him but kept taking one more the next night. He also remembers an inflammation in his nose, thought it was caused by the pills, it was the worst bleeding he has had in his life. He stopped talking to people because of his bleeding; he had to use some napkins to avoid staining his shirt.

The worst thing was that he started noticing at the same time the black curtain in his eye, and thought it was because of the pills and the bleeding. The blood was thinning because of the pills and it produced the detachment. Later on, he found out it was a detachment, but at the time blamed the pills directly. Jeremy took a couple of pills more anyway; something strange happened, the symptoms of cold disappeared immediately. It meant that all the bleeding and discomfort had an end the consequence was the retina detachment, of course.

Losing sight in his eye happened in three or four days, Jeremy got a black curtain in his left eye. He remembers reading a newspaper in the cell one morning and having difficulty reading small letters, had to get close to the newspaper and find some source of light. He only had a peripheral vision towards his left side, the center and right side of his vision was black. Jeremy spent lots of time looking at his black curtain in front of a source of light. He saw interesting figures inside it, they looked like small cells one beside the other, each cell having some kind of hexagonal pattern, it was the retina touching the eye. Some days he saw figures resembling a cauliflower with beautiful arrangements psychedelics.

He mentioned his eye problem to the commander in chief and he didn't care, "I think you are OK, you speak, you walk and you eat. Don't worry too much."

"Have you ever heard about the book 'Through the Looking-Glass' by Lewis Carrol?" Jeremy asked Charlie. He was planning to read the book because of his detachment while at Beach Town. He was now looking through a looking-curtain instead. He was legally blind in his left eye those days, luckily had no need to read or write or to drive a car. He started to get worried about the detachment because everybody said better go to the doctor as soon as possible, "You can become blind if you don't, people said."

Charlie told Jeremy that he had read about the detachment of retina on the Internet and the recommendation was to act as soon as possible, "Listen, as soon as you get a break, go to the capital and find some medical help."

Because of medicine and food scarcity, Jeremy also blamed the government. He didn't find pills for his high blood pressure and cholesterol, and it was difficult to find pills for a common cold. He thought the lack of high blood pressure medicines could cause his eye to explode and produce the retina detachment. He asked doctors later on about detachment of the retina. They said it was more hereditary or age related than anything else, but he still has his doubts. Another thing he remembers is suffering a blow in his left eye during a squash match many years ago; maybe it was that history of events, followed by cataracts, that made his eye weaker. There is a point in time, after so much suffering, when people get obsessed with the relationship between their ailments and the government.

He was in prison for more than two weeks, it seems rebels took back the town and there was a possibility of getting free. The rebel commander was a mature man and it seemed very empathetic toward dissidents. The next morning, all prisoners were aligned outside the cells. The commander was reviewing one by one the credentials of prisoners, left by the government military. When Jeremy's turn came up, the commander said that his face was familiar and asked him where did he live when he was a kid, at about 10 years of age. Jeremy responded saying that he lived at the Capital, in the neighborhood of Saints Bernard, near Precious Mountain.

The commander said, "My name is Wilson, I lived in that neighborhood when I was a kid, show me your right forehand." Jeremy showed his scar and the commander said, "Wow, it is you, Jeremy, we played together and you came to my pool. Nice to meet you again, long time no see."

Later that day, the rebel commander Wilson told him, "According to government records, you have been participating in a plot to get rid of the President. I suggest you not to get back to the capital while the President is still in power, it seems there is a martial law down there and you are in danger. However, I congratulate you for having the endurance to fight intellectually against this regime. Patriots like you are the ones our country needs. People that publish their ideas and let the world know what is going on in Small Venice. Do not forget to mention me in your writings."

He thanked Commander Wilson and assured him a written note on his new book projects. He was free again it is so sweet to be able to move wherever you want. Jeremy was not going to forget Commander Wilson anymore, he gave him lots of advice on how to proceed in the future showing a deep knowledge about the problems of the country. He recommended to leave the country in case of having some family outside, the following years were going to be too harsh to stand by.

Jeremy went back to the house and checked the food leftovers. Eggs and vegetables were rotten, but cassava and cookies were still intact. He put the rubbish in a bag and put it outside. He went for groceries again, bought just a few things for a day or two. He was decided to go back to North America with his daughters, Wilson told him several times to do that, he didn't want to become legally and actually blind. He had to move fast, the situation in the country was difficult. He found out that on the East side there were some airports working. He couldn't go back to the capital, the government would execute or put him back in prison; he didn't appreciate his first experience in jail. He started to make some arrangements getting access to the Internet and using his phone. It was a miracle that those services were still available with a war going on.

He found out which airports were open and he was able to make a reservation to fly in a few days. He bought his flight ticket by the Internet, paid with his international credit card; he had to wait only a couple of days more to fly out. He took a bus toward the East side to one of the big cities. There were military personnel on the way but he didn't have any problem on the road. Flying back to North America was an adventure, stopping first in nearby airports and then waiting a day or two for the connection. The socialistic regime is expert in making life hard for all, not only for

SOCIALIST BINGO - Germinal Boloix

rich people but for everybody, including the untouchables, poor people he meant.

He had laser surgery as soon as he went back with his daughters. Laser surgery requires a gas bubble inside your eye, to keep some pressure in the retina, to keep it in place. The gas injection is painful but is just one shot. The gas stays there for at least seven weeks; Jeremy looked at his world through the gas bubble. A couple of days later he had laser surgery, which is quite painful, equivalent to 30 gas injections. The laser is like a welding machine, the tear is repaired and the retina is put back in place. Jeremy was in shock after the operation, felt like vomiting, like needing to go to the bathroom, didn't find a good position sitting down and was crisped. Because the operation was late in the afternoon, Jeremy and his family were going to have dinner in the way back home, a couple of hours driving.

He said in plain shock, "Please let's stop at the drugstore, I need some painkiller." He got a couple of painkiller pills and waited inside the car, alone, before going for dinner; after 20 minutes he started to feel better and he entered the restaurant to join his family and grab some food.

In the next appointment, after the operation, the doctor said, "The bubble is your best friend, keep resting as much as you can on your right side, such that the bubble keeps the pressure on the retina." It is almost incredible to find out that a relatively simple operation, though painful, makes you weak, and that you need lots of rest to get better. Jeremy was resting for 6 weeks, most of the time laying on his right side; he watched TV or slept; his wife was helping him all that time, she was his guardian angel. He didn't walk outside his home for several weeks these were hard times for him, no exercise at all. He resisted well before starting to get better. He went outside just on few occasions. After two months he started to perform most of his normal activities.

His vision was improving over the weeks, but after seven weeks, he still saw the images in his left eye smaller, compared to the right. With a little bit of imagination, Jeremy can write a new book, 'Through the Looking-Gas.' Jeremy expects to get new glasses in the following weeks because he needs to start his normal activities: reading and writing his books. He has already started some activities, such as walking, getting groceries, reading email, doing payment transactions on the Internet, writing some book paragraphs, and so on.

The reasons of detachment are not clear, according to most doctors, it is most probably relied upon aging, also cataracts. Jeremy had cataract surgery in his left eye about 20 years ago and also in his right eye, 9 years ago. Another reason for detachment, Jeremy thought, was because of a virus. Jeremy started to investigate on his own and found out that the eye is one of the areas of the body not rigorously patrolled by immune system cells or perhaps the initial reactions to the virus cause inflammation that damages organs such as the retina. He was convinced the virus was the cause of his detachment independently of what the doctors said.

Lack of medicines for blood pressure and cholesterol were less lightly to be the cause of detachment. Food shortages or a harsh diet wasn't either. The fault is governmental, they stopped the productivity in the country. However, all these difficulties are manifested in several ways and impair the population; some because of bad services, others because of delinquency, still others because of the economy, and so on. It's not fair to let people suffer for so many years just because the government wants to stay in power. The new socialist government has not been capable of solving food and medicines distribution shortages; it is a regime that deserves to disappear.

Now, from a safe home in North America, Jeremy listens to Internet radio news and finds out how things are going on in Small Venice. The situation is still the same, a divided country making people sufferers of an non-deserved fatality. The map of the country is divided into four blocks as mentioned before, but there is a new area that wants to separate, it is the Andean Mountains. This is an idiosyncratic region that doesn't appreciate the West petroleum-producing region and want to separate. The Andean Mountains is a very independent and self-sufficient region that has always wanted to function in sovereignty. However, they are fighting for the access to the biggest lake in the world, to improve their commerce.

He thought about the effort he put studying the relationship between a society and a game, and a framework or model to structure that notion. The keywords for a society are justice, production, and prosperity. Justice involves fairness, law, and order. Production includes all the activities required by a society to benefit its citizens, such as supplying food, medicines, transport, education, health, appliances and many other services. Prosperity is a measure of improvement obtained by people belonging to the society. There are actors that belong to the community, primarily its citizens. There are some other considerations such as facilities, technology and recreation.

In most games, there are important notions about rules and justice. Any game has some rules to define its purpose and scope. Notions of justice establish the conditions to win. In all sports, there are referees to

SOCIALIST BINGO - Germinal Boloix

help interpret the rules and make decisions on the events. The concept of production means that there are players acting on the field or the board; they master the results. The fans represent a particular class of actors that may have a say.

An important point to understand a society is to differentiate a socialist or capitalist approach. What makes a socialist society different from a capitalist one? Do they have different objectives? Or the means are different? A society should provide prosperity to their citizens, independently of the political approach. A society that doesn't prosper is condemned to failure.

The objectives of any society should be equivalent, however, according to the political approach there are definitive differences: the individual versus collective viewpoint, the pure financial gain versus the false socialist welfare. There are serious setbacks with socialism: they have not demonstrated anywhere their feasibility yet; socialists societies are usually autocratic, forcing their citizens to follow their orders; collectivities have never demonstrated productivity, instead, they are unproductive; socialists governments manipulate public employees forcing them to obey the orders of the party in power.

Final Notes

This journey has taken us up until the end of the trip, many subjects have been treated, a great deal of distorted knowledge has been shared. Independently of the amount of distorted knowledge discussed, it was possible to clarify many disadvantages about socialism; we are a step closer to define as universal knowledge the non viability of socialism. The distorted knowledge of individuals allows their own interpretation of facts; the arguments were convincing. I hope it was useful; at least we have the opportunity to reflect back with better arguments. Human beings differ more than what we think they resemble.

Jeremy has criticized almost the whole society, nobody gets assured, all are guilty; of course, generalization is not good in every case, but shows the real tendency. Do not forget that Jeremy is an Indigo child, he sees things clearly than other human beings. Because of his sensibility, he felt discrimination directly on top of his skin, he also felt the repression of the regime punishing and killing so many young people that did not deserve to die in those conditions. He knew that socialism was not a solution, it was a shame that people fooled themselves with a political approach with matriarchal and religious tendencies.

The analogy between political approaches and games was helpful to demonstrate how absurd is socialism. Personal interest makes people accept unjust systems, the informal bingo game has demonstrated that tendency. On the other hand, applying ironically socialism to soccer shows how absurd are socialist political strategies in the sport; the same thing happens in a society, implementing socialist has brought ruination in the country, it is a decadent approach that should never been an alternative.

The situation in the country asks to cry one's eyes out, more and more people are expressing themselves by tears, including those affected by tear gas. Jeremy has cried a few times during his life, few times strongly, others lightly and others imperceptibly. He remembers crying strongly when his mother died, 34 years ago, and when he read the book 'The Anne Frank Diary,' one year ago, and found out the infamous destiny of the teenager. Imperceptibly, he has cried several times while watching a film or finding about an unjust event or because of harsh times suffered by a family member. Lightly, he has cried when finding about the death of the little daughter of a friend suffocated in a fire, or finding about the terminal illness of a friend, and a few times because of the country's situation; once he cried at the end of the 70's when he recognized the country was not evolving towards a prosperous society. Actually he cried noticing the immense deterioration affecting the population with Absurd Socialism.

Jeremy's journeys demonstrated with basic arguments that socialism needs to be effaced from the human's conceptual knowledge database. Super-controlling societies don't produce progress. Using the abstract notion of Collectivity to force the individual to lose freedom is nonsense. Collectivity only applies when everybody, one hundred percent, agrees on or requires an alternative; the term group must be used for those approving the alternative and they are the ones affected, everybody else must not suffer any consequences. Stop using collectivity to force everybody to follow the same twisted path.

Intellectuals have not been at the height of the needs of society. It is easily demonstrated that socialism is not viable, but intellectuals have not published the convincing arguments we need. Society requires philosophers taking charge of humanity, charlatans must not be allowed in power. Society complexity must be stratified identifying groups that deserve consideration. Social justice requires each group having real opportunities; up to now, traffic of influence has eliminated equality. Knowledge is important to participate in a just society, where individuals make some effort and accomplish with merits a space in the value chain.

The only Social aspect of socialism is its name. It is not true that socialism is for the good of the poor. The poor get poorer under socialism. Socialists need to manufacture poor people because in other case nobody would support them. The big mistake is generalizing in the name of the collectivity, everybody being equal, everything managed by the State, having a unique truth, and so on. It is scientifically demonstrable the failure of socialism, it is not necessary to try it in practice harming humanity.

Jeremy is just a single case of so many thousands people suffering atrocities through another Socialist improvisation. There have been too many socialist trials in the world, making people suffer so much discrimination and scarcity; it is enough of a lesson for the human race to accept so much injustice. Let us efface the Socialist approach in the universe as a possible solution, it does not work, nobody needs total control of the State. It is clear that people in need are the ones supporting Absurd Socialism, please brainwash yourselves, liberty is more important, socialism is envy to triumph, it crushes everybody alike.

Capitalism, within a democratic society, not being a completely satisfying solution, is still a feasible alternative. There are adjustments to be made in a capitalistic democratic society, to make it a bit more human and productive for the good of the people and not for a small group of money builders. A Social Capitalist Society should be a better solution instead of a retrograded Absurd Socialism.

One important consideration is culture; political approaches must be established to help maintain and improve the principles and values of a society. Culture must evolve at its own pace, it is not a socialist imposition. It is unwise to force a totally different culture on people. Socialism is a totally different approach that does not fit with the culture of our country, it is not viable. Small Venice has its own culture, developed for many years, do not you dare to bother us with useless approaches.

Socialist principles agree with the vision of the poor, "Nobody should be poor even though we all are." Socialists do not accept variety, they do not approve some wealthy and others less wealthy; they do not approve some knowing more than others. They believe human nature accepts being inferior humanly or economically than others. Human nature must be treated with its virtues and defects. People are different, their motivation is not the same, behavior is different; it is not fair to accept a unique world vision that applies to everybody without considering the capacities of each one.

Socialist principles only promote the first level in Maslow Hierarchy, where people live to survive. Of course, survival and laziness are the socialists objectives, no work at all. Socialists promote giving jobs to everybody, even though they are not prepared to perform on them; they believe on flat hierarchies where a laborer can be the manager without the required skills.

Socialists praise the Island's regime without noticing that the Island's revolution did not benefit The People; the Island socio-communist dictatorship transferred the wealth of the rich to its bureaucracy, only the party in power got benefited, The People is still waiting. The same is happening in Small Venice.

About People
- People accept wrong governments for interest, some for money, others for power, others for fame, and still others for stubbornness
- Poor people applauded the loss of purchasing power suffered by the middle class; today they pay dearly for their own loss of purchasing power

SOCIALIST BINGO - Germinal Boloix

- Wealthy people are very arrogant, they do not contribute in the society as they could
- Intellectuals that know about socialist negativity, have not written for the people, they have only written for their colleagues
- People do not understand or study the purpose of life; in the same way people must contribute to the society, they must fight for a just society that it is not socialistic
- People are born with their personality, it is impossible to be changed. That is the reason why people use to say that we are born a liberal or a pessimistic or any other adjective, but knowledge opens our eyes
- Human behavior must be and will be the main determinant to establish an adequate political strategy
- When they wish a change against the establishment, they must not choose utopia, let us be realistic
- Some are not interested in learning, are stubborn, think they know everything; they do not want to make an effort to learn
- People don't care about political ideologies, they only care about survival
- They should look for happiness according to Daniel Gilbert: love, music, exercise and chat, and much more than that
- Most people live day to day without worrying about what happens around
- People don't take the time to read and study the limits of socialism or capitalism
- People want politicians to solve their problems and politicians want instead people solving theirs

About Society

- The objectives of a society must be independent of political approaches; do not let politics interfere with a society well run
- Every society must take into consideration Maslow's Hierarchy to find out how are they doing
- Production and justice should be the main objectives of a society, giving everybody opportunities according to people's capabilities
- Society must consider the individual as the main transformational entity

- Societies must avoid considering collectivity as a unique entity; groups of persons with similar needs must define their own objectives, possibly different than other groups

About Democracy
- It is unjust; the 50%+1 is not a solution to humanity problems
- Must be revised to make it useful
- Allows charlatans to take power
- Popularity Contests must be avoided
- People require much more information to make choices
- It is a beginning, not an end
- Democracy and philosophy must group forces to improve the world

About Socialism
- It is absolutely authoritarian, they force people to obey the orders, imposing their bureaucratic centralized criteria
- It is discriminating, punishing those who dissent of the regime
- There has never been a revolution, the People got carried away by interest and not by conviction
- It is based on envy, take away from the rich to give to the poor; instead of promoting work and merits
- It promotes the criterion that if you have something and I do not have it, then better nobody has it
- It is absurd and ludicrous; examples and experience demonstrate
- It is a shame that intellectuals have been so lazy to show the non-viability of socialism; scientists and philosophers have a golden opportunity to demonstrate it
- It is against freedom
- Work and productivity are not among its objectives
- It does not promote innovation, it is retrograde
- Promotes incapable people, it is not interested in knowledge
- It is not related to helping the poor, as they suggest
- It is a strategy defined by a minority only to take power
- It favors loyalty and minimizes people's merit
- Justice is based in collectives, crashing the individual.
- Collectivization of the society only brings poverty because the initiative of the individual is truncated

SOCIALIST BINGO - Germinal Boloix

- Who establishes collective socialism criteria? A group of bureaucrats!
- Love to control the life of individuals, but the performance of their government is not

About Capitalism
- Includes authoritarian considerations because the entrepreneur hires workers to do whatever he orders; however, it is preferable to distribute the authority among the population instead of concentrating it in a few bureaucrats
- Favors freedom of individuals and enterprises
- Promotes merit
- Requires regulation
- 'Pure Capitalism' goes against prosperity for all
- Pure Capitalism is not going to solve the problems, social strategies are necessary to be incorporated
- A type of 'Productive Capitalism' is required to generate jobs and prosperity for all
- Social Capitalism needs to be defined and proposed

Recommended Readings
- A Theory of Justice, John Rawls
- The Republic, Plato
- Capital, Karl Marx
- On Human Nature, Edward O. Wilson
- The Sane Society, Erich Fromm
- Complexity, The emerging science at the edge of order and chaos, M. Mitchell Waldrop
- Communist Manifest, Karl Marx and Friedrich Engels
- Life is what you make it, Peter Buffet
- Thinking Fast and Slow, Daniel Kahneman
- The Blink, Malcolm Gladwell

Epilogue

The political situation in Small Venice is quite difficult the regime doesn't want to take a step back allowing elections on time to change the President. Not even Lenin would have suggested this immobility, he used to say: first one step back and later two steps forward. The regime keeps going forward to a precipice, the Absurd Socialism is so blind that they don't understand the danger of their stupidity; everybody is going to pay for their incongruity. When the omelet is burning in one side, we have to flip it over, there is no choice. The government must go.

In the last visit to Small Venice in 2017, the situation is even worse, repression is brutal, throwing expired tear gas affecting the lungs and throats of neighbors living near manifestations, of course, the neighbors are going to respond with 'PooTov' bombs; people is looking into the garbage to find food, it has never happened before; people in long lines to buy bread; the inflation is huge, it would be around 800% this year, people need at least four minimum salaries; many food items are not available and those you find are extremely expensive; they want to eliminate the 100 Pesos bill without valid reasons and they do not finish to bring the new bills of 500, 5000, 10000 and 20000 Pesos. The government is into the mud, they go from one problem to the next without solving none.

Repression has been exaggerated, and worst of all, the government has been allowing so many young people killed undeservedly, it would seem the government has some dark interest with so many deaths to keep the power by force. Now, with the story of changing the Constitution they believe they can perpetuate in power; the mistakes of the government have been so evident that they are only going to delay their fall. This repression can be considered as a crime against humanity, punished internationally, the heads of government will be punish whenever they fall, we hope it will happen as soon as possible. Luckily, up to now, a military coup d'etat has not yet happened; in case of happening it would mean a bloodshed.

The military would be happy if the predictions of the book became a reality, they would keep their power; it has been their fault, the country follows ahead without direction, they should have been more honest. However, life in the country has the same difficulties of an after war era. And it is clear that war is in the air. People continue their struggle for survival; political freedom and activities are limited, a dictatorship keeps its power and no solution is expected in the near future.

SOCIALIST BINGO - Germinal Boloix

November brought the bad news about the election of 'Blondie' as President of the Giant of the North and the good news of 'Bearded' dying in the Island. Everybody knows that the election of 'Blondie' represents a step back not only for the Giant of the North but for the world. Let us hope it does not mean a third world war. People say that he is not going to comply with his promises, but what would those that voted for him are going to say? About 'Bearded,' his critic is not only because he killed thousands and made suffering millions of people for a bad strategy, but because after more than 50 years in power, there is no definite improvement in his country.

While I was writing the Spanish translation of the book, I had an accident, my computer fall and it did not want to restart. I am lucky to know about computers and I bought a data transfer equipment to copy the data into another data storage medium. Finally, I made a repair on the hard disk and the computer came back to life. It was a relief to be able to continue my work until the end.

www.ingramcontent.com/pod-product-compliance
Lightning Source LLC
Chambersburg PA
CBHW051759040426
42446CB00007B/439